FLAMENCO

For Casten

BARBARA THIEL-CRAMÉR

FLAMENCO

THE ART OF FLAMENCO,
ITS HISTORY AND DEVELOPMENT
UNTIL OUR DAYS

Picture on front of cover: *Angelita Vargas*, bailaora, Sevilla. Drawing by Miguel Alcalá.

Inside of the cover: *El jaleo*. Oil painting by John Singer Sargent, 1882.

Title page: *Cristina Hoyos*, bailaora, Sevilla. Photo by Marie-Noëlle Robert.

Published by:
REMARK AB, P.O. Box 3049, S-181 03 Lidingö, Sweden
Telephone: 46 8 766 50 41. Telefax: 46 8 766 50 42

Translated by Sheila Smith.

Excerpts from "Play and Theory of the Duende" by Federico García Lorca, in Deep Song and Other Prose (© Herederos de Federico García Lorca 1954, Copyright © 1975 by the Estate of Federico García Lorca, Translation copyright © 1975, 1976, 1980 by Christopher Maurer); used by permission of New Directions Publishing Corporation, New York.

First published in Swedish, 1990 – ISBN 91-9712-590-3.
Also published in German, 1991 – ISBN 91-9712-593-8.
Also published in Spanish, 1991 – ISBN 91-9712-594-6.

ISBN 91-9712-592-X
Copyright © 1991 by Barbara Thiel-Cramér and REMARK AB.

Printed and bound in Sweden by
Bohusläningens Boktryckeri AB, Uddevalla 1991

LIST OF CONTENTS

PRESENTATION

Talking about, writing about, thinking about, discussing Flamenco involves entering total, bewildering chaos since the validity of every theory which has been presented about its origin, development and enrichment during the course of this century is dependent on each individual's way of looking at it.

Each of the "initiated" thinks he is right and that is why so many controversies have arisen around this marvelous art, which exists only among the Spanish people.

After reading this book, which Barbara Thiel-Cramér has written with such great expertise, I realized that thanks to her impartial approach and to her own career within the world of flamenco, combined with her relations to, her studies of and consultations with connoisseurs of the essence of this very complex art form, it has been possible to describe its long passage through the time in concentrated form, in a clear and entertaining manner.

All the chapters in this book are interesting because they clarify the author's view of the matter in an apt, easily understood style, using maps, sketches and illustrations.

When I, as a connoisseur of the subject, began to read this book, I did not put it aside until I had finished it, since in a simple and very attractive form the various theories are revived which all my life I have heard disputed by flamenco artists of rank with whom I have cooperated.

The book will be used as an orientation for those who are unacquainted with the background of flamenco art and it will be obvious to every reader that flamenco *exists*, how it was born of a fusion of various civilizations and cultures down through the ages, with the gypsies acting as catalysts. And that this happened just here, on our barren and fertile, frigid and sweltering, religious and pagan, uncommitted and passionate, peaceful and bloody, rebellious and submissive, tragic and joyous Iberian peninsula.

For all of this *is Flamenco*.

José de Udaeta
Barcelona, April 1991

INTRODUCTION

In recent years the word flamenco and all that it implies has attracted an ever increasing amount of attention. The word has a ring of something magical and unknown. It is also a manysided artform which has a fascinating history.

This book is a description of how flamenco came into existence, the historical and social background and the development up to our times of this unique phenomenon called flamenco.

To a great extent I have used Spanish words especially in the flamenco context, the first time *with* translation, afterwards *without*. My intention is to create the atmosphere and maintain all that is enticing and special in the life of flamenco.

The historical information does not claim to do anything other than facilitate understanding of the developments in Spain which produced the art of flamenco.

This book is for those who seek out flamenco for professional reasons, I turn also to those who come into contact with flamenco in other ways: Travelers who have lived in the country for longer or shorter periods as well as all of those in their home countries who would like to get an insight into what flamenco really is.

I have included the description of two Andalusian folk festivals because so much of flamenco's heart and soul finds expression in them. There are strong feelings in both: there is pride, depth, passion and joy, characteristic features of the art of flamenco.

I have received a great deal of assistance and pleasure using Spanish research, chiefly through authors such as Félix Grande: Memoria del Flamenco, part I and II; Ricardo Molina and Antonio Mairena: Mundo y Formas del Cante Flamenco; José Blas Vega and Manuel Ríos Ruiz: Diccionario Enciclopédico Ilustrado del Flamenco, part I and II. Otherwise the reader is referred to the bibliography on pages 143 to 146.

For a long time it has been evident to me that there is a need for information on the subject of flamenco and I hope that the reader will receive the benefit I tried to deliver.

Lidingö in April 1991
Barbara Thiel-Cramér

HISTORICAL BACKGROUND

Iberia, Spain and Portugal, the Pyrenean peninsula, is an almost square land mass surrounded by the sea except for a bit in the north where the Pyrenees mountain chain forms the border with France. The other borders are the Mediterranean Sea and the Atlantic Ocean.

Iberia is the old name for Spain; the original inhabitants were called *Iberians*. Between 1000–800 B.C., the Celts, an Indo-European people, moved westward to Europe and in 500 B.C. they came down to the Iberian peninsula where they mixed with the Iberians. The Spanish sometimes call themselves Celt-Iberians.

Early in history, long before our time, people of different nationalities from the east began to go out to sea, westward. They were bold and enterprising sailors; they wanted to explore the unknown, dangerous ocean and unknown, enticing lands. They came all the way to the Iberian peninsula where they colonized the southern coast. With them they brought the trade and culture of the East. Down through the ages different peoples have contributed to the formation of the character and culture of the Spanish people.

Phoenician and Greek colonies by the Mediterranean Sea 1100 B.C.–500 A.C.

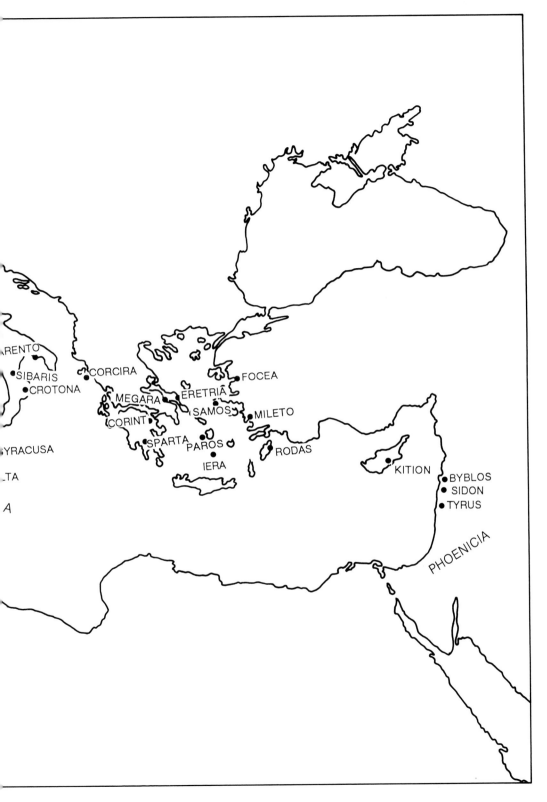

In 1100 B.C. over the Mediterranean Sea from east and south, came the earliest colonizers, the Phoenicians. They were seafaring, merchant people who defied the unknown dangers of the west and traveled as far away as to the Pillars of Hercules, the two cliffs on either side of the Strait of Gibraltar. This was until then the outer limit of the westward voyages of the people of the Mediterranean Sea. The Phoenicians ventured all the way through the Strait and founded the city of Gadir, now Cádiz, on the Atlantic coast in the southwest of Spain. In addition to mercantile goods they also brought with them musical instruments from Tyrus and Sidon.

The legendary rovings and voyages of the ancient Greeks are well documented. Beginning in 500 B.C. they were the next people to come to the coasts of Spain. They founded many colonies deep in the interior of the country. They built temples and theatres and left behind rich treasures in the Spanish earth. One can trace the origin and influence of Spanish dance from that time. On reliefs and bowls, pots and dishes one sees dancing

The first Roman provinces in Hispania, the Roman name for the Pyrenean peninsula, 206–194 B.C.

Bacchanalia, fawns, nymphs, temple girls who twist, glide and swing. One recognizes in their movements the characteristics of the Spanish dance: in the twisting movement — the spiral movement — in the counter movements of the arms and upper body, in the gentle backward bending of the woman's backs and in the position of the head. Castanets, which had come to Greece from Egypt and Crete, would be the most typical accompaniment to the dance, like the participation of the audience through handclapping and shouts. Rome took over the role of the Greeks as rulers of the sea and in addition the Roman Empire spread quickly over large land areas in Europe and North Africa. During the 600 years during which its empire lasted Spain was a Roman vassal state. Many famous men, emperors, philosophers and poets were drawn from this area. Martialis was a poet from Spain who wrote *epigrams* in which he speaks longingly of his fatherland and of the famous and seductive dancers from Cádiz. According to Cervantes they danced with *honey in their hips* and were called *las Andaluces delicias* — the Andalusian delights. He writes of Telathusa, the Gaditian dancer who is said to have been the model for the famous sculpture, *Venus Callipygos*. She is bending backward and turning her head to the side, a characteristic movement in both the Greek and the Spanish dance. These castanet playing dancers delighted the Roman society and the elegant ladies obtained earrings in the form of castanets and chin-chines, small cymbals which were worn on the thumb and middle finger. They sound like delicate bells when they are clapped together.

When the western Roman Empire began to lose its power in the fifth century, A.D., the Iberian peninsula was invaded from the north by the Visigoths. They were a warlike, barbarian people who remained in the country about three hundred years without leaving any clear traces in the Spanish folk culture.

Song and dance were probably not their main interest; they preferred feuds and battles. Many dances in Northern Spain are war and sword dances, some of very early, possibly Visigothic origin. The earliest known folk dance in the whole country is *Danza Prima*, which still is danced today in Asturia.

The jews came to Spain very early. Their period and activity in the country is treated in a special chapter. The most significant immigration was the Arabian-Moorish invasion at the beginning of the eighth century, A.D., an event which played a decisive role in the ethnological and cultural development of the country. This will be described in detail later.

These different peoples, who for longer or shorter periods resided in the country, left traces of their cultures which gradually mixed with that of the native population.

Many came to Andalusia and stayed there. There the song was born, *el cante, el cante jondo*, the deep song which is the beginning and origin of all flamenco. Out of the mixture of the different peoples' music the flamenco song was born and this mixture took place in Andalusia.

THE ROOTS OF FLAMENCO

The Jews

The people who first sailed westward from their homeland and landed on the Iberian peninsula were the Phoenicians and the Jews from the Middle East. They were bold seamen and enterprising merchants. The Phoenician colonization on the south coast of the peninsula is well documented. There is reason to believe that the first Jewish settlements in Spain date from the Phoenician epoch, that is to say at least 1.000 years B.C. According to Is D Abbou's book Musulmans Andalous et Judéo-Espagnols it can be established with reasonable certainty that the Israeli epoch in the country began long before the Christian era.

With time the Jews on the Iberian peninsula became considerably more than a minority of the population. During the fifteenth century there were nearly 900.000 jews who to a great extent were responsible for the prosperity and greatness of the country.

Among the Jews Spain was called *Sepharad*, from which the word *sepharadim* — also sefardi — comes. The Jews in Spain called themselves *sepharadim* and considered themselves superior to their countrymen in Poland and Russia. They claimed that their history was more splendid and more worth while than that of the others.

Miguel Funi, cantaor and bailaor, Lebrija. Drawing by Miguel Alcalá.

The Golden Age of the Jews in Spain can be placed between the eleventh and the thirteenth centuries, a period when they were very well treated. King Alfonso IV was tolerant with respect to religion. Many Jews held high office and even married into Christian families.

Under this king's reign the Jews in Andalusia had been harshly persecuted by the fanatic Almohads, a dynasty from North Africa which ruled the Muslim world in Spain at that time. The king, however, allowed the Jews to move freely and to live in peace and quiet in the Christian provinces in the North. There is a great deal of evidence testifying to their high position, to the respect they enjoyed and to the fact that they received all sorts of privileges.

They helped the Christians with the re-capture of land from the Arab-Moorish empire, most importantly Córdoba and Sevilla. In these two cities the Jewish quarter is the oldest, the most beautiful and the best preserved. In Sevilla it is called "El Barrio de Santa Cruz" and in Córdoba "El Barrio de la Judería".

After the thirteenth century the Christian persecution of Jews began; from then on the dreaded Inquisition struck all heretics. After they had driven out the last remnants of the Moorish empire in Granada, the "Catholic Kings", Ferdinand and Isabel issued a decree ordering all non-Christians either to leave the country or be baptized. As a result of this decree the majority of the Jewish people in Spain emigrated for good.

They always called themselves *Sephardic Jews* and spoke spanish. There are, however, still a few families left in Spain with Jewish blood in their veins, also in Flamenco circles.

The Arabs — The Moors

To the Iberian people the Arab invasion in the year 711 A.D. came like a bolt out of the blue and the conquest was complete by 716.

For roughly a century the Arabs had followed the exhortation of the prophet Mohammed to spread Islam around the world. They expanded rapidly in all directions and one of their routes led westward along the coast of North Africa.

Montgomery Watt says in his History of Islamic Spain:

"Not for a moment was the 'Holy War' solely a religious phenomenon. It was also a political and practical action."

So that the prophet's harbingers should be able to survive and have the strength to endure during their attacks it became necessary for them to carry out raids farther and farther from their bases. All of Egypt fell under Arab rule between 640–643. Despite several counter-attacks by the coastal population the Arabs continued to advance westward. Finally the North African countries, now known as Tunis, Algeria, Libya and Morocco, with their Berber and Moorish tribes, were captured by the Arabs and converted to Islam.

The Muslims (the Arabs and the people of North Africa, the Berbers and the Moors, that is everyone who professed Islam) heard tales of the Iberians' great riches and fabulous treasures. With the help of Berbers and Moors from North Africa and Mauretania the Arabs crossed the narrow strait (Gibraltar) and spread like wild fire over the Iberian peninsula. Without that help they would never have succeeded in this bold enterprise. Montgomery Watt says that it is more correct to speak of the Muslim invasion than the Arab.

As early as 710 a small group of only four hundred men on a reconnaissance expedition had landed in Tarifa west of Gibraltar. The following year a larger contingent of about 7.000 men arrived. Their leader was a Berber named Tarik b. Ziyad, who has given the name to the rock of Gibraltar (Gib = rock; al Tar, Tarik's rock).

The Visigoths, who first occupied and then ruled the Iberian peninsula after the fall of the Roman Empire, had been weakened by internal strife at the time of the Muslim invasion. They offered little resistance and the aggressors were able to advance northward rapidly. Within a short time they had occupied the whole country with exception of Asturia.

Santiago, the first Christian apostle in Spain, came to the country during the first century, A.D. Christianity now spread to the north and by virtue of this faith the kingdoms of Asturia, Aragón, León and Navarra united to drive back the invaders and take back their lands. This event marked the beginning of *la reconquista*, the re-conquest, which was to continue for almost eight hundred years.

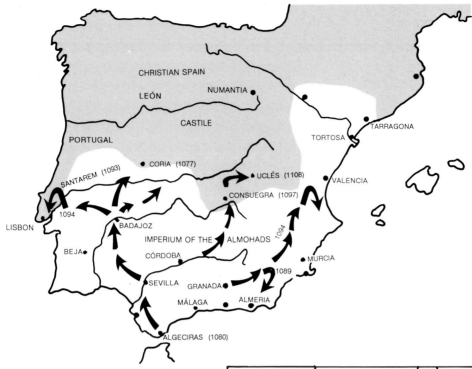

The Arabian caliphate in Córdoba existed from 788 until the 11th century, when Los Almoravides, a dynasty of Moors from North West Africa, came into power. They were succeeded by Los Almohades, a dynasty of Moors and Berbers from North Africa who kept the power until the end of the 15th century, when the Christians gained possession of Granada and so ruled over all Spain.

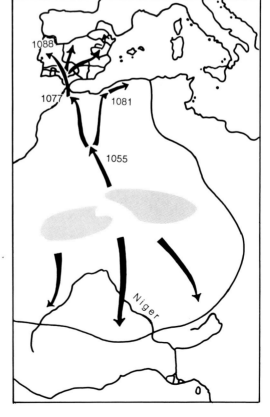

The Moorish invasion of the Iberian peninsula.

For the Muslims it now became a question of rapidly establishing their absolute control of the country. Some of the population in the occupied regions had converted to Islam but not a sufficiently large number to make any difference in the political struggle.

After a series of power struggles between the Arabs and the Berbers a young member of the Omajja family from the caliphate in Damascus, 'Abd al-Rahman, was finally elected its first leader. He was proclaimed emir of Al-Andalus (the Arab name for Andalusia) in the Mesquita in Córdoba in 788. The caliphate in Córdoba was founded during the reign of his successor, 'Abd al-Rahman II (822–852) and during these years cultural life flourished in all forms.

The city became a center of science, literature, poetry and music, attracting students from home and abroad. The Arabs sent for musical instruments from Damascus and Medina, such as the lute, which was to play such an important role in the musical life of Europe during the Renaissance. Musicians and dancers were imported from Bagdad. Magnificent palaces were built; wondrously beautiful gardens with exquisite fountains were laid out; the luxurious and voluptuous life style of the Oriental princes dominated the court.

During the middle of the tenth century 'Abd al-Rahman III (912–961) built the fabulous *Medina Azahara*, a city outside Córdoba, for the enjoyment and delight of the princes. Here the number and luxury of the festivals could be compared to those in Harun al-Rashid's "Thousand and One Nights". It is situated at the foot of *Monte de la Nova*. The ruins of the city, which housed more than 12.000 people, can still be seen today. Most of them belonged to the caliph's guards. The architecture was inspired by the Byzantine, which predominated in the tenth century.

The building of the great mosque in Córdoba, La Mesquita, the second largest in the world (the one in Mecca is the largest) was begun by 'Abd al-Rahman I in 785. It was completed under later caliphs, 'Abd al-Rahman II and III. In 1236, after he had captured Córdoba from the Moors, king Ferdinand built a walled-in Catholic cathedral in the immense columnar forest in the Mesquita. A remarkable mixture of religions and styles.

In the tenth century about a million people lived in Córdoba, an incredible blend of races and nationalities, of folk groups with different life styles, languages and cultures. Jews, Arabs, Berbers and Moors lived separately in their ghettos or districts; others with a higher material standard lived in palaces. Integration between the immigrants and the native population was, however, unavoidable and since that time the Andalusian people have been an indistinguishable union of these races.

During the following centuries music and dance developed from this union.

Córdoba was, at that time a living, teeming city, with a manyfaceted musical life. There were liturgical music from the synagogue, Greek and Byzantine songs, Muslim and Jewish *chants*, melodies from India, Persia, Iraq and North Africa, besides native songs and music. Among the many talents imported by the emirs from Medina, Bagdad and Byzantium there was a singer and musician named Ziryab, known as the "Black Bird" because of his dark skin. He is believed to have come from Iraq. According to Félix Grande he was also an expert instrumentalist. He changed the strings of the lute, which previous to this had been made of silk, to strings from lion gut and he added a fifth string to this instrument. Above all he was a great artist. Legend has it that he knew ten thousand songs. Because of his teaching and his songs he is considered the founder of the National Academy of Music in Spain.

Most of the roots of flamenco can be traced to the rich blend of liturgical and secular music from the East which met the gypsies when they came to Andalusia in the fifteenth century. It was the breeding ground for the continued development and mixing of Andalusian folk music and for the flamenco song.

The Inquisition

Now something happened which was to transform life for the people involved, ruin it for people who had immigrated long ago, for all nonChristians. *La reconquista* — the reconquest — was about to take back the entire country. Montgomery Watt writes that when the Christian troops were victorious in Sevilla in 1248 they couldn't suppress their awe and amazement at the sight of the city's beauty and grandeur. The Christians had never seen, much less owned anything to equal it.

The persecution of the jews intensified. Henry Kamen writes in his *La Inquisición Española* — The Spanish Inquisition: "Finally, in 1391, these tribunals were set in motion with a series of blood baths worse than anything to which the Jews had been subjected to in Spain."

The fanatic, holy faith was supposed to be the driving force behind the Inquisition but the chance to appropriate the Jew's property was also a motive for these bestial actions. The Jews were accused of being traitors, blasphemers, homosexuals, child murderers, prisoners, etc. Those who wanted to remain in the country were forced to give up their own religion and be baptized.

The credibility of their conversion to Christianity was called into question. The Inquisition came into being to investigate into and then check this conversion to an alien religion.

The Inquisition was officially established by papal decree in November, 1478.

Jews and Muslims fled in large numbers; more than four thousand families from Sevilla, Córdoba and other Andalusian cities escaped the long arm of the Inquisition. The first auto-da-fé (burning at the stake) took place in 1481 when six people were bound to the stake and burned to death. All in all nine tribunals were established in several different cities and Tomás de Torquemada, the most notorious inquisitor of all time, started his reign of terror.

The majority of the Jewish and Muslim people in the country had now fled and this population drain had devastating consequences. Culturally, scientifically, economically and socially it was a catastrophe.

García Lorca is quoted in an interview from 1936: "Spain lost a marvelous civilization, a poetry, an architecture, an astronomy, an exquisiteness that was unique in the world."

Anti-semitism increased. On January 2, 1492, Ferdinand and Isabel occupied the city of Granada, the last stronghold of the Moors in Spain. Three months later a decree was promulgated ordering all Jews to be driven out of Spain.

Now the "spiritual" unity of the empire began. This would

be enhanced a few months later when Columbus discovered the New World.

In 1502, the Muslims in Granada were forced to choose between being baptized or going into exile. It was forbidden to speak Arabic, to dress in the Moorish style and to use Moorish names.

Before the Inquisition, before the power of the Catholic Church was total throughout *all* of Spain, during the period when the Arabs and the Moors ruled over half the country, from Toledo and southward, freedom and tolerance shed light on all believers, Christians, Muslims and Jews. Marcus Ehrenpreis writes about Toledo in his book, The Land between East and West: "The Moors allowed those who had received the Word (the Christians) to live in peace; their caliphs and emirs respected the religious freedom of both Catholics and Jews. The Catholics could keep their churches, the Jews could build synagogues. Science and literature could grow on the free ground which lies *between* creeds."

At the beginning of the fifteenth century, the people were roused to acts of violence against both Muslims and Jews by the priest Vincentius Farrer. Toledo's Jewish quarter is assaulted, Torquemada holds his first auto-da-fé in Toledo with Queen Isabel's permission. Moors and Jews leave the city in droves to seek refuge in Andalusia. The once fortunate Toledo, where prosperity and culture blossomed, becomes deserted and poor, (Marcus Ehrenpreis).

The Gypsies

We know that the gypsies' country of origin was India. Research shows that their home region was located in the river valleys around the Indus River and that they belonged to the lowest caste, comparable to "pariahs". It is believed that they were persecuted and harassed by the Aryans—the most influential class in India—and that this was the cause of their rootlessness and their nomadic existence.

According to Fernando Quinones' Las Crónicas del 40 "the exodus of the gypsies from India began in the eighth and ninth centuries. A.D., after which they slowly made their way through Asia and Europe, leaving traces of their race in various places. On the other hand, many language studies suggest that their exodus probably took place around the year 1,000." For several centuries they led a nomadic life in Asia, Europe and probably North Africa. Félix Grande presumes that they were just as badly treated in other countries as they later were in Spain.

An estimated 180,000 gypsies crossed the Pyrenees and travelled down to Spain by stages. Most of them came to Andalusia and they remained there.

There are two kinds of gypsy groups: the nomadic and the settled. It was not by coincidence that the latter, the larger group, ultimately chose Andalusia as their home land. Félix Grande writes: "The strong gypsy-Andalusian symbiosis (fusion) which characterizes the surprising cultural phenomenon known as *flamenco* indicates, or at least suggests, that there are basic cultural similarities between the gypsies and the Andalusian people". Typical character traits such as fearfulness, pride, volatility, resignation and superciliousness are common to both Andalusians and gypsies.

Some researchers say that the gypsies who came to Spain from the south over the Strait of Gibraltar had lived for a while long ago in northern Egypt without, however, mixing at all with the Egyptian people. There is no proof of this theory but it is nevertheless considered true. *Gitano* — the Spanish word for gypsy — is thought to have originated from the Spanish name for Egypt — *Egipto*.

A word which occurs in *el jaleo*, that is in the cries from the spectators which express appreciation, admiration, enthusiasm, is *faraón*, or *faraona*. Pharaoh — in Egypt the highest ruler. There are other signs which point to a connection with Egypt, as for instance: The gypsies are said to have come into the country in the middle of the fifteenth century. In an archive in Barcelona, one researcher, Amada Lopez de Meneses, has found a priceless document from January, 1425. It is a passport or letter of safe-conduct from King Alfonso V in Zaragoza addressed to Johannis de Egipto. Briefly the gist of it is that this Don Juan de Egipto Menor and his followers were to be treated well and were to be allowed to proceed without interference on their journey through

Mario Maya, bailaor. Granada. Drawing by Miguel Alcalá.

Catalonia and Aragón. Those who disobeyed would be subject to the wrath and indignation of the king.

In Andalusia the gypsies found a country which certainly must have been Paradise in their eyes after their long, hard years of wandering. It was a land with a delightful climate, extensive olive plantations, slopes with vineyards, forests, rivers and mountains; a rich land. But they also encountered poverty and misery. The great estates were owned by a few and the people were badly paid or not paid at all and were treated wretchedly. Ricardo Molina says in his *Misterios del Arte Flamenco:* "It was into this miserable and down-trodden proletarian class, reduced to beggary for most of the year, consisting of isolated groups of persecuted people, that the majority of the gypsies established themselves," and he adds, "Something which vaguely resembled class consciousness on the part of the Andalusian proletariat and the persecuted gypsies was to grow into complete mutual understanding."

The early period of the gypsies' stay in Spain was relatively untroubled. The letter of safe-conduct just mentioned and similar permits helped them to move about in the country without unpleasantness.

Apart from Alfonso V's helpful disposition, (his nickname was "El Magnánimo" — the Magnanimous) Christianity in Europe during this period was full of good will and charity toward the wayfarers, penitents and pilgrims who said they were on their way to holy places like Santiago de Compostela, Notre-Dame in Paris or to Rome. The gypsies made the most of this.

The positive attitude of those in power toward "the new people" lasted for the greater part of the fifteenth century. The gypsy chiefs often called themselves *conde* (count) or *duque* (duke). Thanks to letters of safe-conduct *Conde Tomás de Egipto* or *Duque Pablo de Egipto Menor* could travel freely in the country with their people.

But this "honeymoon" couldn't last forever. The diversities in culture and identity between "the Wandering people" and the country's own inhabitants were too great.

Although the gypsies were accomplished and had talents, they also were said to have had a penchant for shop lifting. The resident population began to distrust these unknown, nomadic

undetermined periods of time, far away from home, he went under, not only because of the cruel and inhuman conditions on the ship or in the mine but also because he was alone, without those close to him — his brothers, sisters, parents, grandparents, children and cousins. When he was deprived of the prerequisite for his normal life, his social milieu, he lost his vitality and his will to live. Gypsies prefer to take conceivable punishment rather than be left alone — alone with unknown non-gypsies.

It is not only close relatives who are counted as family. He calls all older members of the clan *tío* and *tía* (uncle and aunt) because they belong together.

"Within the family, behind closed doors, by the light of the oil lamp — *el candil* — he guards the honour of his sisters and daughters, preserves the memory of and respect for his ancestors (an insult to the memory of the dead is a serious offence which calls for severe punishment), is particular about respect for his father and mother, cherishes an unwavering love of freedom, maintains his language, his pride an haughtiness, his faith in his own culture, which is basically a belief in life." (Félix Grande)

The persecutions. These incessant persecutions; three hundred years of continual persecution and harassment. This ought to be enough to break the strongest spirit. But as long as he has his family around him, the gypsy seems to be a pillar of steel. Or perhaps he is as tough as an osier, which bends but never breaks.

THE BIRTH OF THE SONG

As mentioned earlier, the gypsies also lived in a kind of community, partly with the poor rural population in Andalusia and partly with the Moriscos (Christian Moors) who had remained in the country after their supposed expulsion at the end of the fifteenth century.

These three folk groups had a great deal in common: their low social standing; extreme poverty; incessant hunger and their music: the Andalusian folk songs and music; the gypsies' melodies and rhythms; the Moors' North African and Oriental strains, *melismas*. Melism comes from the Greek word "melisma", song. It is marked by the introduction of two or more tones on one and the same syllable, for example the gliding notes which are a distinguishing feature of the flamenco song, such as ay — ay — ay. In the West, melism occurs chiefly in Gregorian chant and folk music from the countries where the influence of Arabic culture has been important. It is even characteristic of Indian art music. Down through the years these kinds of music mingled together and fused and came to be called *gitano-andaluz*, gypsy-Andalusian.

The gypsies, who were most exposed to the hate and unjust punishments of the authorities and the ruling class, began now

Dancing gipsy in the neighbourhood of Granada. Drawing by Gustave Doré.

behind closed doors to give vent to their inner anguish. Their sufferings were given form and content in the songs of lamentation which were the origin of all flamenco. These lamentations were the building blocks on which flamenco was set.

Ricardo Molina says in his book, *Misterios del Arte Flamenco*, "from an anthropological standpoint, as a deeply human factor, as an artistic expression of a collective, *el cante flamenco*, the flamenco song, is a wail of complaint from a people who had been repressed for centuries. Flamenco is the primal scream in its primitive form, from a people sunk in poverty and ignorance. Only their utter need and their instinctive emotions exist for the people." He adds that their songs "are desperation, dejection, lamentation, distrust, superstition, curses, magic, wounded spirit, a gloomy confession from a suffering and abandoned race. Song is self therapy. The tragedy of their song is not theatre or an attempt to impress the audience. It is living tragedy. It is another world."

Félix Grande pictures the slow birth of the flamenco song in this way, "One night, one morning, one dawn, one of these victims of pain and desperation moaned and wailed in a way which was obscurely reminiscent of music, based on an almost imperceptible tradition. It has its origin as much in an imitation of sound, in an outcry, in a gasp of anger and fear, as it has in the influence of the 15th and 16th century Andalusian music.

For a period of two hundred to three hundred years, this roar, this howl of some anonymous prisoner, was repeated, transformed, broadened, concentrated. This form, this organism, now verbal and tonal, has been given a name: *Carcelera* (carcel = prison), the prison song, what is sung in prison. It is a branch of *las tonás*. Las tonás is the first autonomous form of the gypsy-Andalusian song we know of."

Nothing happened during the next three hundred years up to the end of the 18th century. One can suppose that during these centuries the gypsyAndalusian people continued to live their miserable lives, full of privations and punishments, and that their songs of lamentation were their only relief and recreation. A therapy. But sometimes, in spite of everything, the gypsies' sense of humor and feeling for the burlesque doubtless emerged. Now and then they could probably forget their sorrows and banter and joke among themselves.

At the end of the 18th century something happened which gradually made life easier for them. This was also the time when the first songs emerged from obscurity and the first time a singer's name became known outside the inner circle. It was *El Planeta*, the gypsy-Andalusian song's first known figure.

George Borrow, an English traveller and research worker in Spain in the 1820's, says in his book, *The Zincali or An Account of the Gypsies of Spain*, published in London in 1843, that Carlos Tercero, Charles III, king of Spain 1759–1788, passed a law which made certain improvements in the life of the gypsies.

This king, praised by many, strongly criticized by a few who saw beneath the surface, had a single interest in life: hunting. The fact that he should be interested in gypsies was strange and Borrow assumes that the law was the work of some more enlightened person. Although it contained many strange provisions, it was nonetheless a step forward in comparison to the earlier laws. In any case, the king signed it and it is a fact that from the end of the 18th century the gypsies could "come out of their holes" and live in a more open fellowship with those around them.

In the 15th century when the gypsies came to Spain they found other groups who had remained there and settled in lower Andalusia, in Sevilla, Jerez and Cádiz and in the countryside and the villages between these cities. There they found an environment, a mixture of people, which they themselves could be a part of. Besides the original population, the poor country people of southern Andalusia, a large group of Moriscos lived here who had remained after an earlier attempted expulsion. There were also some Jewish families who had succeeded in hiding away in the inaccessible mountains and forests while the Inquisition was at its most violent.

These three groups of people, who had a great deal in common, had merged during the course of centuries. Their cultures had been absorbed into each other, especially in regard to everything that had to do with music. It was this that the gypsies now discovered.

Sofia Noël, a well known Jewish Sephardic singer, suggests, "When we claim that the gypsies created the flamenco song we refer to a relative creation. It was their hidden powers, applied to music, which turned them into jesters, singers and dancers in countries like Russia, Hungary and Spain, countries which for a long time past had their own tangible and typical folk music and dance. What is remarkable and exciting is the discovery that in every country where they remained, they were to interpret that country's special musical character with greater authenticity than its own people. The flamenco song is the result of the various ethnic elements which were magically fused in the melting pot of Andalusia.

The gypsies in Andalusia and *not in any other region* welded song with material which they found in lower Andalusia and initiated the prehistory of flamenco in the 16th century."

What, then, were these materials? Sofia Noël lists these dormant elements which the gypsies encountered in Andalusia: Oriental and Greek influences; songs from the synagogue; prayers and songs from minarets; Greek liturgies; Indian, Persian, Arabic and North African melodies, profane and sacred; Arabic-Andalusian dances and zambras and traditional old dances and songs from Cádiz.

The list is in accord with a classic statement by Spain's greatest musician, Manuel de Falla. He writes, "In the history of Spain there are three facts which are of importance to our culture in general, and of the greatest significance for our musical history:

– the adoption by the Spanish church of the Byzantine song
– the Arab invasion
– the immigration to Spain and the establishment there of numerous bands of gypsies."

All these facts are the roots of flamenco. They are the deep springs out of which the flamenco song, *el cante*, through the poor and downtrodden gypsy-Andalusian people, rose as a new creation, a birth of something new and vigorous. Flamenco, which is song, *el cante*; dance, *el baile*; and guitar playing, *el toque*, is a new art form. It is not an art of the people that just anyone can practice, but a deep personal expression of tragedy, an intense feeling of happiness, a burlesque situation and other emotional experiences which come from the heart and soul. Naturally this demands an artist, man or woman, whether singer, dancer or guitarist.

El Planeta.

The first well known epoch of flamenco's existence dates from 1800 and continues until 1860. This period is called *the primitive or first stage*. From this period we become acquainted with some names of singers. The three earliest were *El Planeta*, *El Fillo* and *Tío Luis el de la Juliana*.

El Planeta is the eldest. He was born in Cádiz at the end of the 18th century. He and El Fillo were the first famous flamenco singers. They were legendary figures and renowned both during their life times and during the succeeding epochs up to the present. Yes, as long as the art of flamenco lives on. Some scholars maintain that he got the name, El Planeta, because he often alluded to the stars in his songs.

El Fillo was younger, probably born in the 1820's. He is thought to have been a pupil of El Planeta's and probably came from Puerto Real, near Cádiz. He has come down to posterity largely because he has given his name to a special type of voice in the flamenco song, *afillá* (the Andalusian abbreviation of afillada). El Fillos voice was hoarse and gruff and since his life time it has often been imitated when primitive, early songs are sung.

Some research workers know of Tío Luis el de la Juliana, others do not mention him. He was from Jerez and was born at the end of the eighteenth century. He was known as an interpreter of *las tonás*. After these three followed a long series of names among the gypsies, both men and women. They always took pseudonyms, like *Juan de Dios*, John of God; *Maria de las Nieves*, Maria of the Snow; *La Perla*, the Pearl; *Perico el Gallego*, Perico of Galicia; *Frasco el Colorado*, Frasco the Red; *Luis el Cautivo*, Louis the Prisoner and many more. Their names have come down to posterity and with them *el cante*, the flamenco song, enters its historical phase.

These singers were exclusively gypsies and they seldom sang for a public outside their own circle. But sometimes, at festivities such as weddings, christenings and other solemn occasions, the gypsies were called in to enliven and entertain the guests with their songs and dances.

In another setting, considerably more extensive, the Andalusian folk songs poured in: jotas from Cádiz (which later became alegrías), fandangos from various villages around Huelva, sevillanas, malagueñas, harvest songs, cradle songs. In contrast to the gypsy songs, these were generally well known and were the property of the Andalusian people.

Diego Regalao, cantaor. Drawing by Miguel Alcalá.

During this epoch, from 1800 to 1860, the first centers for *el cante* were established. The gypsy ghettos, *las gitanerias*, in the big cities of lower Andalusia, Seville, Jerez and Cádiz, were the most important. *Los Puertos* (the ports), Santa Maria, Puerto Real, Isla de San Fernando and San Lúcar also became well known *el cante* districts. Of secondary importance were Ronda, Morón, Lebrija, Alcalá, Mairena and Medina Sidonia. For those who are familiar with the world of flamenco and are captivated by it, these names have an enticing, magical ring. Flamenco artists often take their professional names from the districts where they were born.

Some singers come from Córdoba, Granada, Málaga, but those cities have not been as creative as the places in the Atlantic lower Andalusia. The majority of the gypsies who immigrated settled there. Granada has its special tradition with the Sacromonte Mountain and the gypsy caves. That will be dealt with later on.

The Spanish name for a flamenco singer (male, female) is *cantaor, cantaora*; a dancer, *bailaor, bailaora*; a guitarist (almost only men), *tocaor, tocaora* (Andalusian dialect for *cantador, bailador, tocador*, etc.). The Spanish word *tocar* means touch, affect and play (an instrument). The dialectical names are used exclusively for flamenco artists. Opera singers are called *cantante*, male as well as female. Other singers are called *cantor, cantora* and *cantador, cantadora*. Folk dancers and classical dancers are called *bailarin, bailarina* and *danzarin, danzarina* respectively.

Tatí el Pelao, cantaor, and Juanito Mojama, cantaor and bailaor.

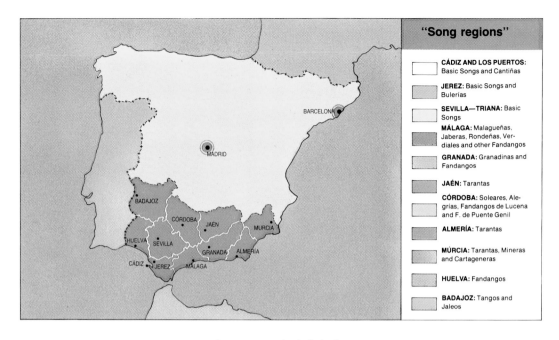

Song regions in Andalucia.

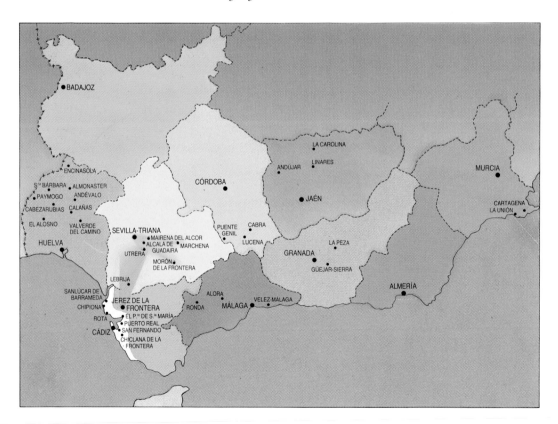

SONG REGIONS

Triana

During the first half of the nineteenth century Triana, *el barrio gitano* (the gypsy quarter) in Sevilla, was the focal point for Andalusian dance and song and for the art of flamenco. Triana is situated on the "wrong" side of the Guadalquivir River. You can walk there from *La Torre de Oro* (The Golden Tower), the twelve-sided tower on the river built as a watch tower by the Moors in 1220, named for the colour of the tiles which at the time made up the facade. One can also imagine that treasures of gold from Mexico and South America were stored there, which Columbus and the other conquerors had stolen during their plundering raids in the West.

You follow the river along the exquisitely beautiful promenade *Paseo de Cristóbal Colón* (Columbus Avenue), pass *La Maestranza*, the most beautiful *plaza de toros* (bullfight arena) in Spain and arrive at *El Puente de Isabel II* (Isabel II's bridge), which crosses the river to Triana.

In Roman times, besides being a trade and shipping metropolis, Cádiz was a song and dance center. The seductive *gaditanians* (the girls from Cádiz "with honey in their hips") are, of course, legendary. Gradually the focal point shifted to Sevilla, which during the eighteenth and nineteenth centuries was *the* seething, incomparable center of Andalusian folk dance and stage dancing.

Serafín Estébanez Calderón, a famous author who depicted the life and manners of his time, was an *aficionado* (lover of) and a specialist in the world of flamenco and its mysteries. Born in Málaga, he lived from 1799 to 1867 and called himself *El Solitario*, the Solitary. He was an inspired story teller. His most famous work is *Escenas andaluzas* (Andalusian tales) published in Madrid in 1847, republished again and again, most recently in 1963 under the title *La Anadalucia de Estébanez*. No one else has had the ability to evoke the atmosphere and the people, the festivals, the intoxicating, intimate mood in the innumerable small tavernas and ventas (taverns and inns) where people gathered in the Sevilla of that time to be together and talk, to drink wine and eat *tapas* (snacks), to dance and sing. He is especially captivated by the *Andalusian* dances. From his famous and much discussed tale "un baile en Triana" (A Ball in Triana) Molina and Mairena quote: "Sevilla is the storehouse for all evocations of this genre, the workshop where the old dances are re-shaped, modified and adapted so that they become something else, something new. It is the university where one learns the inimitable grace, the unequal-

Dancing gipsy, Seville. Drawing by Gustave Doré.

Dance in Triana (Seville). Drawing by Gustave Doré.

led wit and charm, the appealing deftness, the splendid turns, the supple bends of the Andalusian dance.

It is to no avail that new songs and dances of a different, though always lively and sensual character, reach Cádiz from the West Indies and South America. They will never become acclimatized if they do not get rid of the exaggerated desire, the annoying and the monotonous, before they come to Sevilla. When a dance comes into existence and emerges from Sevilla as if from a crucible, pure and clad in Andalusian dress, it isn't long before it becomes known and recognized from Tarifa till Almería and from Córdoba to Málaga and Ronda."

In their book Molina and Mairena stress the meaning

Joaquín el de la Paula, cantaor.

43

El Olé Gaditano. Drawing by Gustave Doré.

and importance of Triana as a center for the art of flamenco. So many well known and famous singers and dancers (male and female) took part in the memorable festival which Estébanez describes that it seems logical to believe that Triana was the great focal point of flamenco life during the first half of the nineteenth century. It was there that the strong power of attraction which flamenco song and dance exerted could be felt and there that all the greatest flamenco artists of the time could be found.

Because of his classic work *Escenas andaluzas* (Andalusian Tales) Estébanez Calderón is regarded as the first *flamencologist*. Today he has many competent and dedicated successors, above all in Spain, who spend time and energy analyzing the concept of flamenco in order to elicit as much truth as possible about this new, fascinating and complex art form.

Cádiz and los Puertos

In the nineteenth century Cádiz was a lively and exiting city. Great Spanish ships carried freight from trade with America and all kinds of goods were smuggled and exchanged between Spain and the Latin-American countries in the west. And not only America. Trading vessels from most of the European countries were to be seen in the ports of Cádiz.

But the great tradition in Cádiz is, of course, as mentioned earlier, dance and song. There was a *barrio gitano* (gypsy quarter) in the city from which many well-known flamenco singers and dancers came as well as from the surrounding ports. Unlike those from Sevilla they did not remain in their home districts but were drawn, like many others with flamenco in their blood, to Triana. At that time no flamenco artist escaped Triana's magic attraction.

Jerez de la Frontera

Sevilla, Cádiz and Jerez all claim to be the cradle of flamenco, and all three cities are, in fact, important names in the history of flamenco. Jerez, of course, is best known as the city of wine. Between the mouths of the Guadalquivir and Guadalete rivers the sweet grape is grown from which the sherry wine with all its variants comes. The great *Bodegas* (wine-cellars) with famous names like Domecq, González Byass, Sandeman and several others are located there.

In the world of flamenco two types of flamenco song can be identified: *cante flamenco andaluz* and *cante flamenco gitano*, Andalusian flamencosong which is sung by a *payo* (non-gypsy) and gypsy-flamenco song which is sung by a *calé* (gypsy).

From Jerez came two giants among *cantaores:* Antonio Chacón and Manuel Torre. The former represents Andalusian song, the latter gypsy song.

Manuel Torre, cantaor.

45

To describe what constitutes the difference between these two song styles is impossible: it must be felt. One difference is that *cante flamenco gitano* (gypsy song) is exclusively made up of the original first songs and the development of these without much influence from outside, while *cante flamenco andaluz* is a song style which began to spread during the middle of the nineteenth century. It is a mixture of different folkloric and musical song styles showing a clear influence of gypsy flamenco. The Spanish inspired songs from South America also contributed to the enrichment of Andalusian flamenco.

These two singers, Antonio Chacón and Manuel Torre, lived and became known during the second flamenco epoch, 1860–1910, the renowned *cafés cantantes* period, which is also called the golden age of flamenco.

Granada

The state of Granada has a special history unlike the rest of Andalusia.

La reconquista — the reconquest — of the whole of Spain occurred in two stages. During the thirteenth century most of Andalusia was recaptured but in the eastern section, with Granada at its center, the Moorish kings ruled up until the end of the fifteenth century, more than twohundred years longer than in the rest of Andalusia. Finally, however, the Christian fighting forces got the better of them and Granada, including the Alhambra castle and the remainder of southeast Spain, was captured by the Los Reyes Católicos — the Catholic Sovereigns — Ferdinand and Isabel, in 1492.

In 1462 gypsy caravans had arrived at the northern border of the state of Granada. There they had paused and eventually followed the Christian advance.

After the occupation of Granada the monarchs immediately had the remaining Moors separated from the Christians. Morerías — Moorish quarters — were established in the Alcazaba and Albaicín sections and a special morería for selected Moors, who were craftsmen and tradesmen, in the lower part of the city, The Christians settled in the central sections.

The gipsy caves in Sacromonte, Granada. Drawing by Gustave Doré.

The gypsies who arrived in Granada consisted of families who had separated from the nomadic tribes. They took refuge in the Moorish quarter, almost as if both races sought each other's company for cooperation and sympathy. The poorest and most densely populated Moorish quarter was on the outskirts of Albaicín outside the city walls near the mosque, which was soon transformed into San Ildefonso Church. In the steep cliffs up towards Sacromonte — the Sacred Mountain — there were many caves. The Moors and the gypsies lived there together until the expulsion of the Moors in 1610. The gypsies, on the other hand, were allowed to remain in the country if they resided in fixed places and if they practiced a trade, for example a craft of some kind.

The origin of the legendary gipsy caves in Granada can be traced to the fact that the gypsies settled in the caves with the Moors and that they remained there for good after the expulsion of the Moors.

Flamenco life in southwest Andalusia was different than that in Granada. In Sevilla, Jerez and Cádiz and the neighboring regions song was the primary form. When the gypsies came to Granada the Moors had been there twohundred years longer

Gipsy dance in Sacromonte.

48

than in the rest of Andalusia. The Moors' primary art form was music and dance. They had their *Zambras*, an oriental legacy from the great caliphates of the tenth and eleven centuries. Zambra is an Arabic word which means sound or noise from voices and musical instruments. It also means Moorish festival with music and hubbub and today it means gypsy festival. José Blas Vega says this in his Diccionario Enciclopédico del Flamenco and he adds that the form of Zambra which occurs today in the caves of Sacromonte is called *la zambra granadina*.

The gypsies took over not only the caves from the Moors but also their music and dance and, in accordance with their disposition and musical talent, described earlier, it was of a stronger and more expressive quality.

Many foreign travelers came to Spain during the nineteenth century, attracted mainly by the romantic and picturesque atmosphere in Granada and Alhambra. The French author, Charles Davillier and the uniquely skilful illustrator Gustave Doré visited Granada in 1862 and became passionately enamoured of the dances in the Sacromonte caves. On one occasion they became so inflamed by the tambourines and guitars that they threw themselves into the dance with two gypsy girls as partners. Davillier describes a gitana, about 15 years old, who danced alone, in this way: She didn't change position, moved only her arms and head, really dancing only with her hips, with great charm and expression.

So the gypsy dance in the caves of Granada has been famous for a long time and many foreign visitors have made a visit to them their most important destination. Earlier, during the eighteenth and nineteenth centuries, it was without doubt a delightful and

Gipsy girl in Sacromonte.

exciting experience. Nowadays — and this has been true for many years — this event, which is still called Zambras, is not always so remarkable.

In 1974, in his book *El Flamenco en Granada*, Eduardo Molina Fajardo writes that in the middle of the nineteenth century there were few singers but fine guitarists. Many famous guitarists have come from Granada and also skilful *guitarreros* — guitar makers — who renewed the art of making guitars.

The art of flamenco in the form which it occurs in Andalusia

Atlantica is rare in Granada and its environs. Dance exists but not the flamenco dance which grew out of song. Instead the gypsies have been influenced by the Arab-Moorish heritage. El cante is not so prominent, while on the other hand guitar playing is rich and varied. There are, however, a couple of songs from Granada which belong to the flamenco group: Granadinas and Media Granadinas.

An event occurred which testifies to the fact that there were forces in Granada which wanted to save flamenco from being wiped out after the decadence at the beginning of the twentieth century.

At that time a large group of artists from the fields of literature and music assembled in Granada—led by Manuel de Falla—a resident. Among the most outstanding of the group's members were Federico García Lorca and Juan Ramón Jimenez—poets; Ignácio Zuloaga—painter; Joaquín Turina, Oscar Esplá and Andrés Segovia—musicians.

It was de Fallas idea to arrange a contest in el cante to inspire undiscovered talents and influence them to sing for an audience and to arouse public interest. Announcements were sent to the surrounding villages in order to gather material in the form of old songs. The contest got under way in an open area in Alhambra on June 13 and 14, 1922. One of those who participated on the first day was Diego Bermudez—El Tenazas—The Tongs—an old singer who had retired after one lung had been pierced by a dagger. When he was told about the contest he walked for three days to get to Granada.

Near the stage were La Niña de los Peines, Ramón Montoya, La Macarrona and Manuel Torre.

Two of the prize winners in el cante were El Tenazas and the promising youth, Manuel Ortega Caracol, eleven years old.

The contest, however, did not immediately have the effect which de Falla had intended: to create a number of flamenco centers and to intensify flamenco activity. The contest was criticized by the skeptical but was praised by others who believed in a future for the art of flamenco.

Nevertheless, the contest had several positive results. First

Manuel de Falla. Oil painting by Ignacio Zuloaga.

the critical and contemptuous changed their minds and began to understand the worth and importance of the art of flamenco and second, because of the flamenco contest García Lorca became strongly committed to Andalucia flamenca. He created his *Poema del cante jondo*, published ten years later and began the preliminary work on *Romancero Gitano* which was to give him his first big success.

Manuel de Falla would certainly have been very satisfied if he had lived to see the consequences of the contest and the subsequent wide spread of the art of flamenco both within and outside Spain.

BASIC WORDS AND EXPRESSIONS

Now it is necessary to clarify and describe (if possible) certain basic concepts within the art of flamenco. What is *flamenco puro*? What is *cante and baile jondo*? What is *el duende*? There are features common to these three concepts but there are also differences. And where does the word *flamenco* come from?

Puro means pure, genuine, unadulterated. It means that the song, the dance, the guitar playing must be genuine, come from within, without conscious effort to make an impression; that the creative artist must sing, dance or play for himself, even with the audience around him; that he be completely committed to his art, deaf and blind to everything else; that he give of himself one hundred per cent.

Hondo or *jondo* means deep, deeply felt. The terms are mostly used about song, sometimes also about dance and guitar playing. They refer to the basic songs, the early, primitive songs of lamentation.

While flamenco puro can also apply to the light, quick and burlesque flamenco, cante y baile jondo treats only the deep, the serious, the songs and dance which comes from the depth of the heart. Here, as in flamenco puro, it is a matter of dancing, singing

Fernanda de Utrera, cantaora and Juan Maya.

and playing for oneself, with a pressure, or force from within.

El duende. The mystical, magical word, often and vehemently debated within flamenco. For some it is almost sacred; others treat both the word duende and the word flamenco a little carelessly without really knowing what they mean.

Federico García Lorca, Spain's great writer, who was shot to death by Franco's men at the beginning of the Spanish Civil War in 1936, quotes Manuel Torre, one of the greatest flamenco singers, in one of his lectures (Cuba, 1930):

> Manuel Torre, who had more culture in the blood than any man I have ever known, pronounced this splendid sentence on hearing Falla play his own *Nocturno del Generalife*: "All that has black sounds has duende." And there is no greater truth.

Lorca continues:

> These black sounds are the mystery, the roots fastened in the mire that we all know and all ignore, the mire that gives us the very substance of art. "Black sounds," said that man of the Spanish people, concurring with Goethe, who defined the duende while speaking of Paganini: "A mysterious power which everyone senses and no philosopher explains."

Antonio Mairena, cantaor.

José Menese, cantaor.

The duende, then, is a power, not a work; it is a struggle, not a thought. I have heard an old maestro of the guitar say, "The duende is not in the throat; the duende climbs up inside you, from the soles of the feet." Meaning this: it is not a question of ability, but of true, living style, of blood, of the most ancient culture, of spontaneous creation.

In the same lecture Lorca describes a scene in a little inn in Cádiz. Here el duende appears in its most intense and violent guise:

The Andalusian singer Pastora Pavón, *La Niña de los Peines*, dark Hispanic genius whose powers of fantasy are equal to those of Goya or Rafael el Gallo, was once singing in a little tavern in Cádiz. For a while she played with her voice of shadow, of beaten tin, her moss-covered voice, braiding it into her hair or soaking it in wine or letting it wander away to the farthest, darkest bramble patches. No use. Nothing. The audience remained silent.

In the same room was Ignacio Espeleta, handsome as a Roman tortoise, who had once been asked, "How come you don't work?" and had answered, with a smile worthy of Argantonius, "Work? I'm from Cádiz!" And there was Hot Elvira, aristocrat, Sevillian whore, direct descendant of Soledad Vargas, who in 1930 refused to marry a Rothschild because he was not of equal blood. And the Floridas, whom the people take to be butchers but who are really millennial priests who still sacrifice bulls to Geryon. And in one corner sat the formidable bull rancher Don Pablo Murube, with the air of a Cretan mask. When Pastora Pavón finished singing there was total silence, until a tiny man, one of those dancing manikins that rise suddenly out of brandy bottles, sarcastically murmured "¡Viva Paris!" as if to say: "Here we care nothing about ability, technique, skill. Here we are after something else."

As though crazy, torn like a medieval weeper, La Niña de los Peines got to her feet, tossed off a big glass of firewater and began to sing with a scorched throat, without voice, without breath or color, but with duende. She was able to kill all the scaffolding of the song and leave way for a furious, enslaving duende, friend of sand winds, who made the listeners rip their clothes with the same rhythm as do the blacks of the Antilles when, in the "lucumí" rite, they huddle in heaps before the statue of Santa Bárbara.

La Niña de los Peines had to tear her voice because she

El Fosforito, cantaor, Córdoba.   *El Chocolate, cantaor.*

knew she had an exquisite audience, one which demanded not forms but the marrow of forms, pure music with a body so lean it could stay in the air. She had to rob herself of skill and security, send away her muse and become helpless, that her duende might come and deign to fight her hand to hand. And how she sang! Her voice was no longer playing, it was a jet of blood worthy of her pain and her sincerity, . . .

Why is the gypsy Andalusian art form, which consists of song, dance and guitar playing, called flamenco? Where does the word come from?

Ever since flamenco research in Spain in the 1960's began to gain momentum at an ever faster pace, this question has been discussed back and forth without having received any conclusive answer. There are several more or less credible theories.

Demófilo, a pseudonym for Antonio Machado y Álvarez, well known ethnologist, a collector and publisher of texts for *el cante*, maintains that the word flamenco as a term for gypsy song originates from two historic events which occurred at the same time: the Spanish king Carlos I (Charles I, 1508–1558), son of the Spanish princess Juana la Loca (Joan the Mad) and Felipe el Hermoso (Philip the Fair) of Habsburg, came to Spain in 1522. There he was called Carlos V (Charles the Fifth). He was born and raised in Ghent in Flanders and felt himself to be more a Fleming than a Spaniard. A court of Flemings accompanied him to Spain, his new country. *A Fleming* is called *un Flamenco* in Spanish.

Angelita Vargas, bailaora.
Drawing by Miguel Alcalá.

At the same time large groups of gypsies arrived and this coincidence — that two groups of foreigners reached Spain at the same juncture — was supposed to have resulted in gypsies also being called *flamencos*. Demófilo can possibly also have confirmed an interpretation of George Borrow's. In his book The Zincali or An Account of the Gypsies of Spain (London 1843) he writes: "*gitanos and egipcianos* (gypsies and Egyptians) are the names under which gypsies in general were known in the past and are still known in Spain. They have also been given other names, like, for example, *castellanos nuevos*, *germanos* and *flamencos* (new Castilians, Teutons and flamencos)" and he adds: "They would probably never have been given the name flamencos if it had not been for the circumstance that they were called, or were believed really to be germanos (Teutons) and that Teutons and flamencos were considered synonymous by the uneducated." This theory coincides with another, namely that the epithet "flamencos" during the time of Charles I had been transferred to the gypsies as an expression of the ill will with which the Spanish people regarded the Flemings. The latter made up the court of Charles I and meddled in the affairs of the kingdom, which was, of course, looked upon with disapproval. This version points up the generally negative attitude towards gypsies, even though they would never have ventured to meddle in the affairs of the kingdom.

Several prominent research workers concur the theory that *flamenco* may originate from slang used at the end of the eighteenth and the beginning of the nineteenth centuries where the word means *farruco*, *pretencioso*, *fanfarrón* (cocky, pretentious, braggart). This meaning still exists. For example, one says today: *no te pongas farruco* (don't be cocky) or *no seas fanfarrón* (don't brag). Today the word flamenco has if anything a positive meaning. If you say that someone is a *tío flamenco* it is the same as saying that he is generous and "go ahead".

THE DANCE

"*Dancing*. There are many the world over who dance well; but those who *walk* best are the Spaniards." So declared La Argentina, the unsurpassed, world famous Spanish dancer to Fernando El de Triana. Because of his pertinent and discerning descriptions of artists within flamenco's three forms; song, dance and guitar playing, Fernando El de Triana is a person of cardinal importance in the history of flamenco. He was from Sevilla and lived from 1867–1940. He was a singer and guitar player. The first edition of his book, *Arte y Artistas Flamencos*, which has proved invaluable to flamenco researchers, was published in 1935. In order to finance the publication of his book a performance entitled *Exaltación de flamenco* was given at the Teatro Español in Madrid on June 22, 1935. On this occasion a great number of poets, authors, singers and guitarists participated, together with a dance group which was led by La Argentina and included other famous names such as La Quica, Frasquillo, Merceditas León and Rafael Cruz. These artists within *el baile* will be described later on.

In about 200 B.C. at the beginning of their period as a great power, when the first Romans came over to Spain to inspect their new conquests, they were impressed and fascinated by the sing-

59

La Tati, bailaora.

ing and dancing young people in southern Spain. They gathered a large group of boys and girls and brought them back to Rome where the gracious and charming girls from Cádiz enchanted the Roman public with their dancing.

The famous *gaditan girls* established early in history Spain's sovereignty as a country of dance.

That's how it was and that's how it is today. Spaniards of both sexes have a bearing, a way of carrying themselves, a natural posture which automatically draws glances to them. Spanish men are famous for their *piropos* — compliments which a woman sometimes receives from an unknown man who passes her and on the way by says in a low voice, for example: *Qué arte de andar* — "Your walk is a work of art" — without any hidden motive. He makes her proud and happy for the rest of the day. Or: rather a long time ago, when *La Telefónica* — the telephone company's headoffice — was Madrid's highest building, a stately Swedish woman was strolling down *La Castellana*. A little man walked past her and hissed through his teeth: *Al lado tuyo la telefónica no es nada.* "Beside you the telephone building is nothing." There are thousand and one piropos, admiring, witty, imaginative, comic. A typically Spanish phenomenon.

Naturally all this has to do with dance, with their interest in and feeling for dance and movement.

Flamenco dance, the genuine flamenco dance, just like song,

differs widely from folk dance and from the large number of classical Spanish dances which existed in Andalucia during the eighteenth and nineteenth centuries. The Oriental heritage is clear. One sees it in the female dancer's gentle, supple arm movements, most importantly the expressive twists and turns of the hands from the wrists. Castanet playing does not belong to flamenco dance although today's flamenco permits castanets with certain dances. Some dancers use castanets in siguiriya, it is quite individual. The men's dance is more austere, with slow, controlled movements of the extended arms; straight, stretched hand, its power and virility wholly concentrated on footwork — *el zapateado* — zapato = shoe.

The guitar is indispensable for genuine flamenco dance and the only instrument which is accepted. Recently the flute and some percussion instruments have sometimes been included but the guitar still always dominates.

The most important and most basic element in flamenco dance is, however, *rhythm*. It gives pulse and soul to the dance; it holds together the diverse elements of a flamenco

Pepa Montes, bailaora.

61

La Chicharrona, bailaora. Drawing by Miguel Alcalá.

dance, varying endlessly according to the character of the dance and the dancer's temperament. There are a great number of flamenco dances whose style and content have developed from the songs. Every dance has its basic rhythm which must be followed straight through but the tempo can be varied with rhythmic adornments. Of paramount importance is the collaboration between dancer — guitarist and singer — guitarist. From the beginning *el cante jondo* was sung without accompaniment. It was sung either *a palo seco* (literally — to a dry stick, meaning rhythmic thumps with a stick which the singer held in one or both hands) or completely without accompaniment. There is no precise information about when guitar playing began to accompany the song, but from the beginning of the nineteenth century the guitar became a part of the art of flamenco and therewith also an active part of the dance. In order to achieve a perfect collaboration between dance and guitar it is necessary for both parties to know their jobs perfectly.

Every flamenco dance or song has its rhythm, its form and structure, which must be followed. It is a common notion among non-initiated that the flamenco is improvisation, that it is free and without rules. It is not so. Every dance has a special form which in certain cases can be strict and firm, in others more flexible and not so marked. But within the framework of form and structure parts of the dance or song can be lengthened, augmented by an element created freely on the spur of the moment, or shortened by the omission of others. It can be varied, the tempo increased or decreased all according to the dancer's and singer's mood and inspiration. It is the dancer or singer who "leads" and the guitarist who follows. What is crucial is that the guitarist is sensitive to and cognizant of certain signals from the singer and dancer which mean, for example, that now he has to finish off or continue. This collaboration is vitally important for all flamenco art and demands long and patient training.

El baile por bulerías — the bulería dance — is a typical gypsy and festival dance which can express the most uninhibited *joie de vivre*, comedy, mockery of oneself and others, jesting and gaiety. In this dance the performer can "spread himself out" in time if he — or she — has the inclination, or shorten the dance to just a few steps.

El Farruco, Matilde Coral and Rafael Negro, bailaores.

Naturally, everything which has been described here means that genuine flamenco dance is a solo dance. In their Diccionario Enciclopédico Ilustrado del Flamenco, José Blas Vega and Manuel Ríos Ruiz quote the following from Curt Sachs' *A World History of Dance:* "Flamenco dance is an individual dance, whether it involves a man or a woman. The introduction of couples is an unplanned consequence of staging. No flirtation occurs, no gallantry as in folk dance. It is an introverted, introspective dance without major transfers in space and without jumps. Danced in a small area with a sort of heaviness and a tendency to direct the movements downward, it is an abstract dance, without theme, without story line. It is governed more by each interpreter's emotion and thus provides some chance for personal improvisation."

El ambiente — mood, atmosphere, milieu — is a highly important ingredient in *el flamenco puro*. In order to experience real *flamenco puro* it is necessary to have *ambiente*, which means that the whole

Antonio, bailaor.

La Chicharrona, bailaora, Antonio Mairena, cantaor and Tía Juana la del Pipa, bailaora.

65

performance ought to take place in a small, intimate place, either private or in a tavern of some kind; that most of the listeners and onlookers are *aficionados*, initiated into the secrets of flamenco; that they are favourably disposed to the artist and that they look forward with warmth and interest to enjoying his or her art. A seething expectation must vibrate in the air. Of course, one can experience genuine flamenco under less ideal conditions, but it is rare. Only in the *ambiente* described above can the flamenco artist do himself complete justice and indeed surpass himself. García Lorca's description of the incident with La Niña de los Peines in Cádiz is proof of how the audience can influence the artist.

The listener-onlooker role is very important. The singer/dancer receives strong support from the intense concentration of the audience and from their positive participation in what happens. They stimulate and animate the artist with *palmas* — hand clapping — , *pitos* — snapping the fingers — and other rhythmic sounds. *Palmas* is a difficult skill which few master to perfection and those who do not should best refrain from attempting it in serious flamenco. The gypsies are masters of this art.

El jaleo — from the verb jalear = stimulate, encourage — is a series of spontaneous, admiring and encouraging shouts from the audience which plays an important role for the singer/dancer if they come in the right place. On the other hand in the wrong place they can be irritating.

As mentioned earlier the art of flamenco has many forms. The genuine flamenco which has just been described is difficult for foreigners to come into contact with. Flamenco folk consider that no one outside their own circle, not even Spaniards, completely understand their art. When an outsider is in the audience the artists usually do not give their best.

But there are other forms which are also flamenco though on another level. In Spain's larger cities there are *tablaos flamencos*, night clubs with a stage and with contracted flamenco artists. — Tablao, a platform with a wooden floor. These *tablaos*, which began to appear in the 1950's are a direct continuation of *Los cafés cantantes*, 1860–1910, the second era of flamenco, called the golden age of flamenco. A detailed description of this period and the change it meant for the art of flamenco will follow later (page No 79). *El tablao flamenco* is a form which does not have the idealistic proportions of the genuine flamenco but where one can still witness very fine flamenco art. Sometimes, however, the quality of the song or dance can be rather mediocre.

A third form of flamenco can be seen in night clubs and on variety shows in the numerous tourist resorts which line the coast of the Iberian peninsula. These feature smaller groups of dancers, singers and guitarists who travel around and perform for an audience which consists for the most part of people who are either seeing flamenco for the first time or who have returned with great enthusiasm in order to understand and learn more. These flamenco groups often consist of three male and three female dancers, one or more singers and one or more guitarists. The beautiful, colourful, sweeping, flounced skirts and shawls of the women are in marked contrast to the austere, elegant Andalusian suits of the men. They often give high class performances. For foreigners the dance is naturally the most attractive and the easiest to understand; the song is more difficult. One has to learn to appreciate it. The guitar playing is almost always first class. The quality of the programs varies. They consist of ensemble dance and couples dance but seldom solo dance. The footwork, castanets, *palmas* — hand rhythms — everything technical — is often of virtuoso caliber, attesting to long years of training. But it can easily be a bit superficial and mechanical.

To come to the essence of flamenco art — it is this:

When the artist is in his own group, first within the family, later on in his circle of friends and *aficionados*, when he or she is allowed to sing or dance on his/her own terms, when inspiration comes, when the spirit and the urge moves him, when *el duende* is present, the art of flamenco reaches its greatest heights. Then nothing can stop it, the audience falls dead silent; the magic power of *the demon* fills the room.

This is *flamenco puro*, rare but real.

The other forms of flamenco are equally legitimate. They have to exist and they can be highly enjoyable.

THE GUITAR

The guitar came to Spain via an instrument resembling the *laud* — lute, which was introduced on the Iberian peninsula by the Muslims during the twelfth century. The name *guitarra* is derived from the Greek word *chitarra*. A guitar-like stringed instrument came into Europe with the Arabs during the seventh and eighth centuries, A.D. The name occurs in thirteenth century Spanish fiction, where it is sometimes referred to as *guitarra morisca* — Moorish guitar, sometimes as *guitarra latina* — Latin guitar.

From these instruments *la vihuela* emerged during the fifteenth century. It acquired the same status at the Spanish court as the lute was to be given at courts in the rest of Europe. The vihuela also existed in a popular variation which came to be called guitarra on the Iberian peninsula. Henceforth the guitar became the Spanish instrument of accompaniment to folk dance and song and later the preferred flamenco instrument.

A special technique is used in flamenco playing — *rasgueado*, also called *rasgueo* = scratch, itch — executed with four or five fingers, which rapidly pluck the strings. Another characteristic feature of guitar playing for flamenco is that *falsetas* occur — short melodies which are played between the songs or dances as filler. Falsetas are very tradition bound, and it even happens that a guitarist asks to borrow, that is take over, a colleague's falseta.

For a long time guitar playing was only an accompaniment to song and dance but as such it was of great importance. In order to do himself justice it is absolutely necessary for the singer or dancer, regardless of the quality of his art, to have a good guitarist at his side. This, of course, goes without saying but during the first primitive stage, 1800–1860, when the art of flamenco began to take its first steps before the public, there was a shortage of guitarists who "knew the art" of accompanying correctly. Guitar playing developed and improved and gradually the first guitar soloists emerged. Guitar playing acquired the same prestige as song and dance. The result of this was that too many guitarists wanted to devote themselves to solo playing instead of accompaniment, not least because of better remuneration, higher status and less work at rehearsals. There wasn't room for everyone and the guitarists took all kinds of tricks to draw attention to themselves like playing with the guitar behind their backs or over their heads and similar stunts. Since that time really skilful and devoted accompanists have become rare. A good one has to be acquainted with and indeed know *all* the songs and dances in order to follow

Justo de Badajoz, tocaor.

Enrique de Melchor, tocaor.

along and help in a satisfactory way. Sometimes he even has to lead his singers and dancers. Ever since guitar playing became as an important part of the art of flamenco as song and dance, there have existed, and exist today, many talented, artistically advanced and skillful solo guitarists within flamenco; strong, creative personalities who have broken new ground for guitar playing. Some of these artists will be described in a later chapter.

FLAMENCO FORMS

What is it like to see and hear flamenco for the first time? How does it feel, what does one think? Does one feel and think anything at all? Best is to be lucky the first time, to see and hear something good. The first impression is important for the continued appreciation and understanding of the art of flamenco. If it is a mediocre or perhaps downright bad (there are such) performance, it isn't possible to become absorbed in it and it can take time to change one's negative opinion. For a non-Spaniard it is, of course, a matter only of the dance and the guitar playing; at the beginning one doesn't understand the song at all.

But dance, guitar, rhythm (*palmas, pitos, zapateado*) put you under their spell, rouse and elevate body and soul so that the surrender is total. A glorious experience. Later it is difficult to try to express in words what it is you have seen and heard. That there are so many types of dances and songs, from the heavy, serious, introverted to the light, happy, humorous and burlesque types, remains to be discovered. It takes time. It is necessary to see and hear a lot of flamenco often and ideally to have access to someone who can answer all the questions which crowd into the mind.

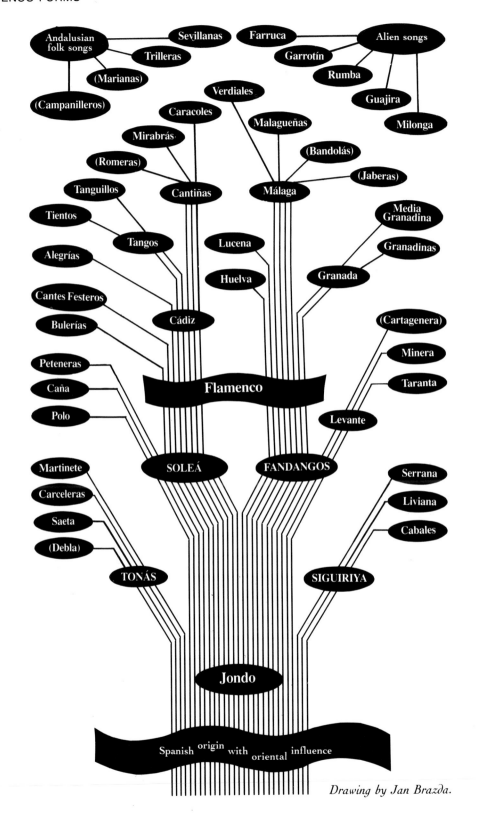

Drawing by Jan Brazda.

Here follows an account of the most important songs and dances and their development from the early, deep —*jondo* — songs of lamentation, the birth of flamenco — from the enormous spread and alteration during the nineteenth century down to the flamenco of today. To make the continuity clear some of the Spanish flamencologists have drawn a classic tree in order to elucidate the origin and the relationship. The tree divides the songs into three groups: *Cantes Jondos* — the deep, primitive basic songs, *Cantes Flamencos* — the lighter songs, and *Cantes Aflamencados* — flamenco influenced songs — songs and dances from outside, from other regions and countries and old Andalusian folksongs. The third group includes *Farruca* and *Garrotín* from Galicia in northern Spain, *Rumba* from Brazil, *Guajira* from Cuba and *Milonga* from the Argentine.

The earliest gypsy songs were *las Tonás* — from *tonadas*, later *tonadillas*. From the seventeenth century all popular songs and ballads from the various regions in Spain were called tonadas and tonadillas.

In his collection of tales, *Escenas Andaluzas*, Estébanez Calderón mentions *las tonadas de Sevilla* which he heard from the gypsies in Triana (Sevilla). According to Molina and Mairena it cannot be ascertained that these songs were to be found there before the nineteenth century but judging by the texts and by the old-fashioned features of the songs, they seem to come from a far away time. Their spiritual world is that of a people who were persecuted and harassed, with prison a constant threat: the Andalusian gypsies' world up to the end of the eighteenth century.

CHART SHOWING THE RELATIONSHIP AND DESCENT OF THE MOST IMPORTANT FLAMENCO SONGS

Denominations used in the text		*Alternative denomination*	
Cante jondo	– deep song basic song	Cante jondo	– deep song basic song
Cante flamenco	– the lighter songs	Cante intermedio	– intermediate songs
Cante aflamencado	– Andalusian folk songs and alien songs.	Cante Chico	– small song

The information about flamenco's growth and furcation during the nineteenth century is for the most part drawn from Ricardo Molina's and Antonio Mairena's book *Mundo y Formas del cante Flamenco* — The World and Forms of Cante Flamenco.

Las tonás are sung *a palo seco* without marking any rhythm with *palmas* or *pies* — hands or feet. Out of this form were born many songs like *Martinetes* — songs from the forge, and *Carceleras* — songs from prison. These early basic songs are difficult to perform and are seldom sung today.

Saeta is a liturgical *toná* which is sung at Easter during the processions, when images of the saints are taken out of the churches and borne on catafalques through streets and squares, night and day, uninterruptedly, from Holy Thursday to Holy Saturday. Saeta is a solo sung voluntarily, spontaneously, from some balcony or street, by some anonymous person among the spectators watching the passing procession. It deals with Christ and *La Virgen* — the Virgin Mary — and their sufferings. It is a strange experience to hear, without notice, a saeta for the first time. The murmur from the crowd ceases; no one moves except those in the procession which slowly advances, only the tense, sharp, naked solo voice cutting through the air and surrounding the holy images.

The most well known and most important type of *jondo songs* is *Siguiriya*. The word is believed to have originated from *La Seguidilla*, a popular folk dance — couple dance from La Mancha, first noted during the fifteenth century, for example in the writings of Cervantes. The word was changed in gypsy dialect to *Siguiriya*. It is usually called *Siguiriya gitana* — gypsy siguiriya — in order to distinguish it from *La Seguidilla*, with which it does not have the least similarity. The gypsies created the Siguiriya, modelled after the first primitive songs, as still one more expression of their tragic and bitter existence during the period up until the end of the eighteenth century. This song has survived all alterations, has been and still is today the most powerful of *cantes jondos*. The Siguiriya has a completely unique rhythm, a monotonous rhythm, which the guitar keeps throughout the entire song or dance. The basic rhythm alternates between 3/4 and 6/8 time and it is difficult for the uninitiated to hear where it begins and where it ends. The great *siguiriya cantaor* Manuel Torre, a gypsy, defined the song as *soníos negros* — black tones. Since the time of the *cafés cantantes* it has also become a dance, but it is only the most outstanding singers and dancers who can execute this difficult *cante y baile jondo y puro.*

El paso de la Siguiriya

ENTRE mariposas negras
va una muchacha morena,
junto a una blanca serpiente
de niebla.

   Tierra de luz,
cielo de tierra.

   Va encadenada al temblor
de un ritmo que nunca llega;
tiene el corazón de plata
y un puñal en la diestra.

   ¿A dónde vas, siguiriya,
con un ritmo sin cabeza?
¿Qué luna recogerá
tu dolor de cal y adelfa?

   Tierra de luz,
cielo de tierra.

The passing stage of the Siguiriya

Among black butterflies
goes a dark-haired girl
next to a white serpent
of mist.

   Earth of light,
sky of earth.

She is chained to the tremor
of a never arriving rhythm;
she has a heart of silver
and a dagger in her right hand.

Where are you going, siguiriya,
with such a headless rhythm?
What moon'll gather up your pain
of whitewash and oleander?

   Earth of light,
sky of earth.

F. García Lorca
Poema del Cante Jondo

Translated by Carlos Bauer.

   A somewhat lighter form of the siguiriya is *Cabales*, which has a quite different musical style. *Serranas* and *Livianas* are other variations, the former a song from the mountain regions, strong and tranquil, a song for men, the latter is short and light, an introduction to serrana.

   La Soleá, from *soledad* — loneliness, belongs to the world of the *jondo songs*. It is a gypsy song, as distinguished as the Siguiriya. It expresses melancholy and pain over loneliness — in the mine, in prison — over lack of love and companionship. As a dance it is proud and noble, uniting power and passion with a clear, pure form. It requires dancers of high artistic integrity.

Now the trunk of the "tree" divides and branches out in two directions. The one side has Soleá as its point of departure for the pure gypsy songs. The other branch has the Andalusian flamenco songs like *Fandangos*, *Malagueñas*, *Verdiales* and *Granadinas*, as well as *Cantes de Levante* — songs from the Levant. These arose and took form in the mining region around Almería, Murcia and Cartagena.

From the time of the Soleá and thereafter the *dance* comes with great vitality. And as the epoch of the *Cafés cantantes* begins, dances spring up like fresh shoots out of the fertile flamenco earth.

La Caña — the name is believed to originate from the Arabic *gannia* — song — has an emphatic and unmistakable introduction, with otherwise the same accompaniment as Soleá. The singers and dancers seldom utilize it. *El Polo* is a daughter song of La Caña, *Peteneras*, a song and dance like a slow lamentation. The words tell of an unhappy woman named *La Petenera* who danced in *El Café del Burrero* (Sevilla).

The songs and dances which are vividly realized are *Los Cantes Festeros* — festival songs, that is, songs and dances at all festivals of rejoicing such as weddings, christenings, birthdays — name days —. They are also used as a general expression of high spirits and extravagance in merry company. An unavoidable feature of these celebrations is, of course, wine, as in all flamenco. In the front ranks we have *La Bulería*, a dance in which the gypsies, even sometimes *payos*, give generously of themselves. When spirits are at their peak the most fantastic configurations and farcical sorts of buffoonery and burlesque can be seen and heard. The bulería also lends itself admirably to making fun of the many current songs and ditties floating around. The guitar is rapid and rhythmic in 3/8 time together with *palmas*, *jaleo* and an atmosphere of high spirit in the audience.

The word *alegría* means joy and that is exactly what the song and the dance convey. Carlos Almendros writes of Alegrías: Las Alegrías is the most important kind of *Aires de Cádiz* — melodies from Cádiz. They are an expression of the gaditanian optimism which breaks forth in the presence of a landscape in eternal balance. It is an invitation to smile and live: white — the salt, blue — the sea. Characteristic of Las Alegrías is finesse and grace. The guitar accompaniment is brilliant, likewise the dance, which, according to Almendros, is one of the most difficult to perform. There is a marked difference between Alegrías as song and Alegrías as dance. The song is happy, full of life, often virtuoso. As a dance it follows the tempo of Soleá but with a certain difference in rhythm and tempo. It is a dance for women, elegant, both solemn and lively with great variation of *el zapateado* — the footwork. If it is well performed Las Alegrías exhibits an admirable combination of rhythmic movements and footwork.

Tangos or *Tangos flamencos* is the oldest form and expression of the genuine "gypsy mirth". It has nothing to do with the Argentinean tango except that it is a dance in two-step. *Tanguillos* is a lighter form, likewise *Rumba flamenca* or *Rumba gitana*, very popular among both its practioners and the audience.

Tientos is a slow tango. *Ir con tiento* — go forward cautiously. It has a lyrical and romantic character, sometimes called flamenco *sentimental*.

Cantiñas with songs and dances like *Caracoles*, *Mirabrás*, *Romeras* are classed as *Aires de Cádiz*. They also have the carefree, light-hearted mood which is characteristic of the gaditanian temperament.

The second branch of the tree has *El Fandango* as its point of departure. It was originally a dance, of Arabic origin, to which the song was added later. As a dance it is prevalent throughout the whole country. There is a Fandango in practically every region in Spain. But as every regional dance has its own style, the Fandango reflects the caracter of each region and has changed accordingly. The best known of these is the Andalusian. In Andalusia it became the eighteenth century dance and song *par preference* — preferred above all others. There are now two kinds of Fandango:

    a – *Fandangillos* (a variation of Fandango), of the popular and local type like *Fandango de Huelva, Fandango de Lucena* and others.

b – Fandangos re-created to a form of flamenco like *La Malagueñna* and *Los Verdiales*.

A large group of Fandangos belong to group a. Molina and Mairena enumerate a total of thirty districts, each one with its own Fandango. Group b consists of the growing and important group of Malagueñas, which at the beginning was a simple Fandango from Málaga. Nowadays the Fandango, together with Verdiales, is counted among the flamenco songs. From Granada emanate the *Granadinas* and *Media Granadinas*.

From the first stage of the art of flamenco, 1800–1860, every *cantaor* and *cantaora* has made certain songs his or her specialty. Some became great interpreters of Siguiriya, others preferred Soleá — mostly women, several became famous for their *Cantes de Levante* — songs from the Levant. The Fandango now also became the favourite song type of some singers. Almost every singer has Tangos, Alegrías, Bulerías and other festival songs on his repertory.

The songs from southeast Spain, Cantes de Levante, from Almería, Murcia and Cartagena, are songs of lamentation from the lonely and heavy work in the mines. They are *jondo* songs. They have a curious, alien sound, gruff and a little harsh, completely unlike the other jondo songs. They are *Tarantas*, *Mineras* — mina = mine, and *Cartageneras*.

Alboreá is a song which is almost sacred to the gypsies. It is sung only within the family, at weddings and christenings. It would be a sacrilege to "release" it to the outside world. For this reason it is not included in the world of Flamenco, though as song it is supremely flamenco.

FROM CAFÉS CANTANTES
TO OUR DAYS

Cafés cantantes = song cafés. Some researchers put the time of their inception, rise and fall in the period 1847–1920; others restrict the period to 1860–1910. Obviously the heyday of flamenco, its golden age, was short and intensive. As early as the final years of the nineteenth century decadence had already begun to set in. But by then a revolution within the art of flamenco had taken place.

From the end of the eighteenth century when the first singers, both male and female, began to make themselves heard, to the 1840's, there were only a few people outside their own circle who knew about the songs of the gypsies. The gypsies, of course, created an absolutely new style and form of song, differing widely from the old folk songs familiar to everyone.

El cante could be heard only in certain small taverns or privately among the gypsies themselves. No one then had any thought other than that the singers sang when they were in the mood, when the pressure from within and the atmosphere around them generated these unknown songs. — But there was to be a change.

José Blas Vega writes in his book, Los Cafés Cantantes de Sevilla: Los Cafés cantantes, which existed between 1847 and 1920, arose for logical reasons out of two circumstances: on the one hand the rise throughout Europe in the number of cafés with musical and variety shows of different types, not only for entertainment but also to satisfy an artistic-cultural need; on the other hand the necessity to canalize the vigorous spread of the Andalusian folklore. In the main the new stage art, *cafés cantantes*, was born of this merger.

Café entertainment had certainly existed before this. The *Escuela bolera* was greatly appreciated. Phillip V had introduced Italian ballet masters in the eighteenth century. They were fascinated by the Andalusian folk dances and brought to them their classic ballet technique and style. The result was escuela bolera — bolera from the word volar = fly — which demanded trained professional dancers. In the eighteenth and nineteenth centuries there was a large repertory of such dances. The Andalusian songs and tunes were also popular in the cafés.

But the audiences began to tire of these programs and the moment was now at hand for the entry of a brilliant flamenco singer by the name of Silverio Franconetti. He had a keen instinct for the commercial and realized that the gypsy song, el cante, could be an appropriate attraction for the cafés.

Before the epoch of the flamenco song in the cafés, *el baile* — the dance — was, as mentioned earlier, a very popular and greatly appreciated feature of café programs. During the entire nineteenth century and even later there existed a number of *academias de baile* — dance schools — where the pupils learned the native traditional folk dances as well as escuela bolera, where all the steps and figures had names, as in classical ballet. These steps were an integral part of a large group of dances which demanded a great deal of training in order to achieve the combination of lightness, elegance and grace with technical proficiency. The café owners went round to the dance schools, selected the best dancers and gave them contracts. Song and guitar playing accompanied them.

The first cafés with cante were rather insignificant. Fernando el de Triana informs us of the first known café cantante, established in 1842 on Calle de Lombardo in Sevilla. He also mentions a few more in Sevilla. They did not last long, disappear-

The Hispanic Society of America, New York. Sevilla, Baile. Oil painting by Joaquín Sorolla.

ing after 1850, but as time went on one café after another arose. In total there were sixtythree cafés in twelve cities; twelve in Sevilla, five in Jerez, three in Cádiz, four in Puerto de Santa Maria, five in Málaga, eighteen in Madrid, one each in Granada, Barcelona, Bilbao, Córdoba and La Unión and eleven in Cartagena. This according to Félix Grande. Other researchers have other information and mention several different cities and towns with cafés.

There is no exact information about what took place in los cafés cantantes up until 1880 when Silverio Franconetti, enormously talented, intelligent and intuitive, opened his own café in Sevilla, thereby initiating the culmination of the epoch. His mother had gypsy ancestors; therefore as a child he heard the old *cantaores gitanos* — gypsy singers — first and foremost El Fillo, whom he had listened to in Triana. So his art had gypsy origins.

In 1856, he traveled over the Atlantic to South America. He spent eight years in Montevideo, working in times of peace as a tailor and sometimes as a *picador de toros* — the horseman in a bullfight who sticks his lance into the neck of the bull. In war time he served as a soldier in the Republic of Uruguay. However, the pressure of the song within him, his inner unrest and his need of freedom brought him back to Spain in 1864. At that time he sang in many cities around the country, chiefly in Andalusia and was an ardent propagandist for the art of flamenco. (Félix Grande.)

And now the change occurred. Silverio was the first

Rosa Durán, bailaora. Oil painting by Augustín Hernández. Private collection, Madrid.

Café cantante. Oil painting by José Llovera. Museo de Arte Moderno, Barcelona.

to truly realize that the time was ripe for el cante; now people would learn to know these songs, which hitherto had led such a hidden, almost secret existence with a small, devoted audience. Silverio engaged certain singers for his café, gave them contracts, arranged the times for their appearances, saw to it that they turned up and that they carried out their duties.

This was no easy thing for gypsies who were used to a free life and to singing when it suited them, not when the audience expected it. The new situation has two sides. They had the security of receiving a guaranteed income — at least periodically — but they also had to conform, to be on time and perform their art when the manager and the audience demanded it.

Silverio was not a bad protector of his gypsy singers — at that time almost all *cantaores* were gypsies — but it is known that the whole thing did not always function so perfectly. He, Silverio, was sometimes forced to jump in himself and appear on stage.

Silverios renown as *cantaor* grew. But for the gypsies it was still impossible to imagine a *payo* — a non-gypsy — as a cantaor, a payo who sang tonás and siguiriyas. It was difficult for them to accept this fact. An old gypsy woman found no criticism other than to shout: You sing fine, but you have awfully big feet. (Félix Grande).

Fernando el de Triana writes of Silverio: "He was the artist I appreciated most; because Silverio was the only cantaor who knew all, absolutely all the songs and he sang them extraordinarily well."

Lorca pays tribute to Silverio in a poem:

Retrato de
Silverio Franconetti

Entre italiano
y flamenco
¿cómo cantaría
aquel Silverio?
La densa miel de Italia
con el limón nuestro,
iba en el hondo llanto
del siguiriyero.
Su grito fué terrible.
Los viejos
dicen que se erizaban
los cabelos,
y se abría el azogue
de los espejos.
Pasaba por los tonos
sin romperlos.
Y fué un creador
y un jardinero.
Un creador de glorietas
para el silencio.

    Ahora su melodía
duerme con los ecos.
Definitiva y pura.
¡Con los últimos ecos!

(Poema del Cante Jondo)

Portrait of
Silverio Franconetti

Between Italian
and flamenco,
how would he sing,
that Silverio?
The thick honey of Italy,
mixed with our lemon,
traveled upon the deep wail
of this singer of siguiriyas.
His cry was terrible.
Old timers say
that one's hair
would stand on end,
and make the quicksilver
split in the mirrors.
He would go up the scales
without his voice cracking.
And he was a creator
and a gardener.
A creator of arbors
for the silence.

    Now his melody
sleeps with the echoes.
Final and pure.
With the ultimate echoes!

Translated by: Carlos Bauer

Besides the *Café de Silverio*, which became the most famous café during the palmy days of the epoch, there were in Sevilla *Café Burrero*, *Café Filarmonico* and many others.

Félix Grande quotes Pepe el de la Matrona, a cantaor from

Dancing in Café Novedades in Seville. Oil painting (detail) by Joaquín Sorolla.
Banco Español de Crédito, Madrid.

Sevilla, born in 1887. Pepe describes the interior of one of the cafés. "There were stalls with arm chairs as in the theatre, rows of chairs, on the backs of which were fastened little tables. Anyone who sat in a chair then had a little table from the back of the chair in front. There he placed coffee, which at that time cost thirty-five céntimos, and his wine glass. There sat the workers who saw the performance at least once, paying thirty-five céntimos. In addition there were boxes higher up around the stalls. Anyone who took a box doubtless knew what it entailed; he had to order one or several bottles of wine and if it was a party of four or five persons many bottles were consumed... until they got warmed up and picked artists to continue the party after the performance in reserved rooms with more wine, song and dance.

Four Performances a day were given in these cafés and it was routine for the artists afterwards to continue their work in the reserved rooms by singing and dancing for 'los adinerados'—the well-off. The 'reserved' rooms were a significant feature of the cafés cantantes during the height of their existence. The café owners did extra business there and the artists could add to their incomes."

In general the decor of the cafés was rather alike except in regard to size, which varied: a wide salon decorated with mirrors; posters with typical popular motifs like bullfighting; *Torre del Oro*—the golden tower; *La Giralda*—the cathedral tower—and the like, heavy drapes, an atmosphere of somewhat artificial luxury. There were small tables and chairs in some cafés instead of arm chairs in rows, a platform for the artists, plus the boxes and rooms for private *juergas*—flamenco style carousals.

The Café de Silverio was a little different. It opened in 1885 on the Calle del Rosario

Bailaora. Oil painting by Joaquín Sorolla. Museo Sorolla, Madrid.

in Sevilla and was installed in a typical Sevillan *patio* with a fountain in the center, columns in Moorish style, everything decorated with brightly coloured tiles. *El tablao* — the platform — was in the patio and also a bar for wine and other alcoholic beverages. The tables and chairs were placed in the arch of the columns and in the upper part of the courtyard one flight up there was an arcade with a balcony parapet; from this arcade one had access to the "reserved" rooms.

The flamenco group on the platform resembled very much those which appear in the *tablaos* of today: one or two guitarists, *bailaoras* and *bailaores* — more of the former; *cantaores para baile* — singers for the dance — and *cantaores* who sang solo with the guitarist. The artist's salaries varied according to their popular appeal but at the beginning it did not exceed ten pesetas a day. How far that would go is difficult to say but it isn't unlikely that it was on the low side even for those times. Antonio Chacón, a famous singer, payo — non-gypsy — was the first to receive twenty pesetas a day. For their salary they often worked until four in the morning, giving several performances in a row.

Pepe el de la Matrona recalls the Café del Gato — The Café of the Cat — in Madrid at the beginning of the twentieth century. "In this café, which was very small, we had to go on stage four times: at the beginning to sing with the women in the *quadro* — the group — in order to become accustomed to and learn the 'craft'; next to sing some verses, and then to sing solo. When I sang a solo one woman was placed at my left and one at my right and then there were the two guitarists; later on we performed in *los quartos* — the private rooms. There were times when we finished at 12 o'clock the following day. Then at our own expense: *aguardiente va y viene* — brandy all round. At eight in the evening we were back again. You could crack from this."

A hard life awaited those flamenco artists who were employed at the cafés cantantes. An advantage was that they could eat every day; the disadvantage was that the quality of the performances deteriorated. For *el cantaor gitano* the insistence on his performing at fixed times with a prescribed program was completely destructive. The basic contradiction between *el flamenco* and *el café cantante* was, it can be said, that the singer was torn between his impulsive temperament and the enforced disci-

pline. The nature, origin and violence of the songs, their emotional abandon, the singular circumstance that the moment of deep insight occurred when the singer himself felt it deeply, all these things point to something elementary in the gypsy personality and explain his aversion to rules and regulations. One can take the position that the existence of los cafés cantantes certainly was good for the spread of el cante, but also that it was detrimental. Javier Molina has simply and expressively pronounced the difference between el café cantante and the tavern or the private home: "It was the opposite of today; earlier the cages were poor but the birds better; now the cages are much finer but the birds are worse." That the birds warbled without inspiration was also perhaps due to the fact that the cages were too fine.

Anyway, the art of flamenco began to penetrate the consciousness of the people; it became known first in Spain and gradually in other countries around the world, in spite of the fact that at the end of the 1890's strong criticism was directed at it by *la generación del 98* — the '98 generation. This was a group of elderly, reactionary authors, poets and intellectuals who condemned flamenco. They declared that it had nothing to do with art and looked down on the professional singers as being commonplace amateurs. Their contemptuous and inimical attitudes were succeeded, however, by understanding and sympathy on the part of the younger poets and authors.

But still, there are clear signs that Javier Molina was right about his birds; toward the end of the 1890's a weariness, a decadence, could be noted. Flamenco was losing its bite and clarity, which was really understandable considering the unwillingness of the gypsies to "obey orders." The economic benefits of their work had become too important. Eventually a lack of renewal was apparent.

But while the art of flamenco was in danger of being reduced to banality in the cafés, one had, however, to thank them for several decidedly positive consequences.

Now it was time for *el baile* — the dance — the flamenco dance, to take its place on stage in *los cafés cantantes*. Before this only the classical dances from the bolero school had been seen,

Matilde Coral.

but now *el baile* followed in the footsteps of *el cante*. and the dances from private gypsy festivals and from the tavern were introduced in the cafés. *Tangos, tientos, zapateados, bulerías, alegrías* became greatly appreciated features for the program. For the "ordinary audience" = flamenco uninitiated, the dance, with its rhythm, movement and sensual radiance was easier to perceive than the song. *Siguiriya, soleá, petenera, caña* were also included in the café repertoire. During this stage of the art of flamenco *dance* grew in importance and acquired the same prestige as *song*.

Guitar playing now became an important part of flamenco. From having been an accompanying instrument it was gradually transformed to a solo instrument. But, as has been mentioned earlier, this fact became a source of rivalry between the players, which could assume ridiculous and disgraceful proportions. When Paco Lucena, a guitarist of great ability, began to play at the Café de Bernardo in Málaga during the café cantantes epoch, Paco el Aguila, the cafés first guitarist, became annoyed at the enthusiastic applause his rival received from the audience and the following episode took place: One evening Paco el Aguila pulled a glove out of his pocket, put it on his left hand and accompanied the singer in this way. A moment later Paco Lucena pulled his chair up to the ramp, took off one of his socks with studied seriousness, put it on his left hand and performed a guitar solo. Félix Grande relates this episode in his book and calls it stupid and grotesque. It nonetheless illustrates the competitive fury of the guitarists at this time. One can imagine what intrigues must have lain behind the advance of the guitar to the front line. But despite these absurd forms they nevertheless helped to spread knowledge of flamenco and its artists. It is one thing to point out the fact that the cafés cantante period produced many fine, skilful solo guitarists — Ramón Montoya, Luís Molina, Habichuela el Viejo, Manolo el de Huelva, Javier Molina, to mention only a few — but it is another not to forget how essential the art of accompanying singers and dancers is. An able and committed accompanist is "worth his weight in gold".

Now the change within the art of flamenco continued. The cafés cantante epoch continued into the twentieth century,

Cristina Hoyos.

Domingo Manfredi Cano says in his book Cante y Baile Flamencos: "Song loses in depth what it gains in breadth." That is exactly what happened when flamenco stepped on to the theatre stages and — incredibly — into the bullfight arenas. The popular culture and the distinctive cultures of the various regions became the objects of a new theatre form: folkloric performances with music, song and dance, scenery and costumes, with motifs from different areas of the many rich national cultures in Spain. The most popular motif was Andalusia with *el cante y el baile*, with exotic Moorish features, with bars and taverns and lots of wine and many jests. Neither cante jondo nor flamenco puro existed here but the happy, light genres like tangos, alegrías, bulerías abounded, together with light parodies of *andalú* — Andalusian dialect — and jokes with the gypsies.

Music-hall songs and revue tunes came into fashion; flamenco faded away on the stages. The cafés cantante epoch ended around 1910 and from 1920 on variety shows and revues took over public interest up until 1955 — with a break for the Civil War, 1936–1939 — when *los tablaos flamencos* inaugurated the rebirth of flamenco.

A strange phenomenon was *Opera flamenca* — 1920–1936 — performances with cante, baile and guitarra, which took place in the bullfight arenas in many cities. No researchers touches on the problem of acoustics. One wonders how singers and guitarists could be heard in these spacious arenas under the open sky with the primitive amplification equipment of the time. But clearly it functioned and the performances became very popular. The great artists joined the tours: La Niña de Los Peines, Manuel Torre, Antonio Mairena, Manolo Caracol and other well known names. In the Opera flamenca, however, the program choice was of lower quality. The public wanted music hall songs and revue tunes and the artists had to sink their artistic level considerably.

The whole of the 1940's, after the Civil War and during the World War then in progress, was a difficult time for the artists; for everyone else as well. Cultural life came to a standstill, jobs were scarce, many were fearful. Flamenco had been forced to

El Güito.

although in weaker forms, but after 1910 new paths were sought.

The theatres and *las plazas de toros* — bullfight arenas — became locations for flamenco performances. The cafés cantantes period was past; it had contributed to the spread of flamenco and its task was completed. A similar form of the flamenco art was to arise fifty years later in the form of *tablaos flamencos* — night clubs with flamenco-shows.

return to its earlier haunts, to the small *ventas* — inns — on the outskirts of the cities where wealthy people could reserve private rooms and engage artists to entertain them with song, dance and guitar playing.

Not until several years into the 1950's could any change be perceived. But then, gradually, something happened which would transform and renew flamenco life. The latest great invasion of Spain — tourism — had begun. With the end of the war, people longed for sun and warmth in new countries where these life-giving forces could be enjoyed. Toward the middle of the 1950's the tourist flood had gotten under way; building started along the coasts and on the islands in the Mediterranean; the small fishing villages were transformed into beach resorts with huge hotels which were rapidly occupied by shops, restaurants and night clubs. Now life began to brighten for the flamenco artists. Small groups began to tour and perform for the tourists. In the cities the first tablaos flamencos opened. These two events are treated at the end of the chapter "Dance".

The first tablao flamenco which opened was *Zambra* in Madrid, famous during its existence as a stronghold of pure flamenco. There Rosa Durán, one of the finest bailaoras of all time, ruled like a queen. Her guitarist was always the superb Perico el del Lunar — Perico with the birthmark. The room for the spectators was long, narrow and intimate, decorated in slightly Moorish style, with a narrow, deep stage. On the stage at Zambra, as in every other tablao, the dancers, singers and guitarists sat in a half circle at the back. One after another the bailaoras rose and performed a fandango or tanguillo, then came a bailaor who danced a farruca or zapateado, a dance of the light genre, to the accompaniment of song and guitar and palmas. The first part of the performance usually ended with sevillanas — the Andalusian couple dance. This was the prelude to the highlight of the

La Argentina. Drawings by José Clará.

Argentina

J.C.

Córdoba

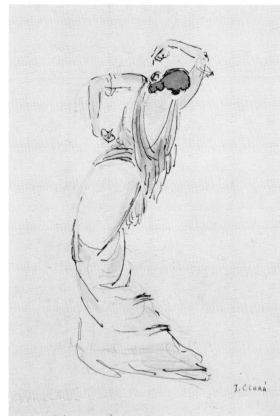

Argentina

J. CLARÁ

. CLARÁ

orrida

E CLARÁ

program which everyone was waiting for; the great artist with singers and guitarists. Rosa Durán took her place on the stage with unsurpassed authority, concentration and radiance. She performed the prodigious, heavy jondo dances like siguiriya, soleá and peteneras with an intensity and simplicity which concealed the technical difficulties and held the audience spellbound. You forgot everything in the presence of this vision of body and spirit. This was flamenco in its deepest and purest form. She also inspired her singers and guitarists to first rate performances. After this monument of flamenco art it was always an anti-climax when the first group came in again. But the mood would improve and finally the whole group would be dancing bulerías in a storm of palmas, zapateado, song and guitar.

The form of the programs of tablaos flamencos came into existence during the café cantante epoch. Zambra set the tone for all the new tablaos which developed but there were few which reached Zambra's level. The quality varied and the artists did not always belong to the front rank. It was therefore important to find out for oneself where the best ones could be found. This was the case from the beginning of the tablaos flamenco's existence and it

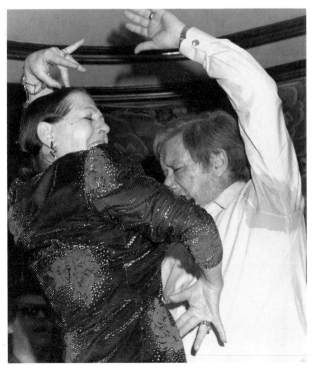

96   *Mercedes León and Albano de Zuñiga.*   *Manolo Vargas and Roberto Ximénez.*

still applies today. As the development of flamenco looks today — 1991 — it is likely to apply for a long while to come.

For young prospective flamenco artists it was, and is, a splendid school sitting with the group around a star. They receive a thorough training in every branch of the art, not least achieving mastery of palmas — the virtuoso rhythmic accompaniment. Every famous singer, dancer and flamenco guitarist of today has sat in the background at different tablaos for one or several periods, learning discipline and familiarizing himself or herself with all of flamenco's secrets.

Zambra's golden days ended when Rosa Durán was no longer present, but it has apparently resumed activity again. Another famous tablao is *Corral de la Moreria* in the old section of Madrid. It has a first rate stage with a Goya motif as a backdrop. Lucero Tena, a famous bailaora, bailarina and castanet virtuoso, was *primera figura* — the solo artist — there for many years — 1961–1984. She toured in many countries, received many prizes in competitions but always returned to the same tablao.

A recent star at Corral de la Moreria was *Blanca del Rey*. She is a marvelous bailaora with a strong personality and great originality. She is famous for her soleá with el Manton de Manila — the enormous shawl from Manila — where she dances with it as if it were a partner. It swings around, it embraces her, it spreads out in big patterns and it clings to her, a magnificent, extraordinary experience of beauty. She also has other choice dances in her repertoire like Alegrías, Guajiras — with fan — and la Caña; long fascinating, extremely personal dances. The great opportunities for individual interpretations of the famous dances and songs are indeed demonstrated here.

Café Chinitas is an elegant tablao in the heart of Madrid with a rather large stage, mirrors and ornaments, polished surfaces. The artists are specially selected and in beautiful, lavish costumes they present a program of the highest quality. A famous star at Chinitas is la Chunga — she who danced the rumba flamenca barefoot.

Other tablaos in Madrid are: Las Brujas, Los Cabales, Corral de la Pacheca, Torres Bermejas and Venta del Gato.

Most of the larger cities have tablaos of varying quality. One must inquire if one wants to find the best.

LEADING ARTISTS OF
YESTERDAY AND TODAY

If all the flamenco artists, more or less famous, who have lived down through the years, added to the new, young artists of today, were to be described and reported on, this book would be twice as thick as it is. Fernando el de Triana mentions and goes on to describe one hundred up to 1940; consequently none of the young and more recent artists are included. Other researchers report on more than a hundred artists.

Here, however, only the most prominent and famous are discussed — those who have enriched flamenco with their art and personalities and gone down in history. Also the prominent talents of today have been given a place, those who want to influence the old, traditional flamenco by rejuvenating it with modern technical innovations within music. It remains to be seen where this "trend" will lead.

Singers

The three earliest known names of cantaores — singers — are *Tío Luis El de la Juliana* — Uncle Luis, son of la Juliana — 1760–1830; *El Planeta* — the Planet — 1785–1860; *Diego el Fillo* — Diego, the son — 1800–1860. At the end of the eighteenth century these three gipsy singers took flamenco's first step into history.

Tío Luis was from Jerez an is said to have sung well all the songs of the time. He was also *maestro* — a teacher — of most of the singers of the next generation.

El Planeta was from Cádiz and is said to have believed in the magical power of the stars and planets. In his songs he alluded to the cosmic powers. He worked in the forges of Triana and was probably the originator of the song style of the Triana school. Picture on page 37.

El Fillo was the most famous of the three and gained immortality because of his special voice. It was gruff and coarse, ideal for cante jondo and it came to be called *voz afillá* after his name.

Silverio Franconetti, 1831–1889. This inspired singer deserves yet another mention; therefore a quotation from Fernando El de Triana below:

"Born in Sevilla, grew up in Morón de la Frontera, of Italian origin; he was the artist I liked best; Silverio was the only singer who sang all, absolutely all songs, extraordinarily well.

Caña

El que siembra en mala tierra	He who sows in poor soil
qué fruto espera cogé;	what can he expect to reap;
que el trigo se vuelva piera	the wheat turns to stone
y no puea prevalesé.	and cannot ripen.

All the songs flowed out of the great Silverio's throat, steeped in honey, with a pharaonic charm and elegance. No one listened to him without a shiver and tears welled up in the eyes of ninety percent of his listeners. This was the great Silverio with his superior voice, gruff but mild as honey from Alcarria."

Juan Breva, 1835–1915. He was king of classical mala-
gueña song and as such the only singer who had the great
distinction of singing in the Palacio Real de Madrid itself — the
Royal Palace in Madrid — in the presence of Don Alfonso XII
and Doña María Cristina. Juan Breva became rich and died
poor — the fate of many singers — so poor that it can be said that
toward the end he sang to collect money for his funeral.

García Lorca describes him:

Juan Breva tenía
cuerpo de gigante
y voz de niña.
Nada como su trino.
Era la misma
pena cantando
detrás de una sonrisa.
Evoca los limonares
de Málaga la dormida,
y hay en su llanto dejos
de sal marina.
Como Homero cantó
ciego. Su voz tenía
algo de mar sin luz
y naranja exprimida.

(Poema del Cante Jondo)

Juan Breva possessed
the body of a giant
and the voice of a little girl.
His trill was like nothing else.
It was that same Pain
being sung
behind a smile.
It evokes the lemon groves
of a sleepy Málaga,
and in his wail there are
aftertastes of sea salt.
Like Homer he sang
blindly. His voice possessed
a touch of sea without light
and squeezed-dry orange.

Translated by Carlos Bauer

Mercedes la Sarneta.

Mercedes la Sarneta,
1837–1910. She was from Utrera, a little village near Sevilla,
from which many flamencos
have come. Fernando de Triana
describes her voice as a beauty
which stunned nature itself and
comments as follows on the fara-
onic style of her *cante por soleá* — soleá song: "Her voice had
an incomparable mildness. Between the shivers her voice

101

evoked, and the maidenly beauty of her face, there was only the fragrant wine from Jerez and the classic Manzanilla wine from Sanlucar."

He writes this poem to her: Picture on page 106.

Cuando murió la Sarneta	When la Sarneta died
la escuela quedó serrá,	the school closed
porque se llevó la llave	for she took with her the key
del cante Soleá.	to the song of Soleá.

Antonio Chacón, 1865–1929. One of the great singers and the first who demanded and received twenty pesetas an evening. Until then no one had gotten more than ten. Chacón was payo — a non gypsy — and the first who sang cante flamenco andaluz. See the Chapter "Song Regions — Jerez de la Frontera."

Manuel Torre, 1878–1933. This gypsy was tall, as high as a tower = torre, and he was without equal as a singer of el cante gitano — the gypsy song. He and Antonio Chacón were the two great names during the best days of the café cantantes. He was a strong individualist who paid no attention to conventions and public taste. A master at expressing agonizing suffering and despair, as well as refreshing good cheer and joy, he sang when he felt like it with wild duende. Picture on page 45.

Pastora Pavón — La Niña de los Peines — The Girl with the Combs, 1890–1969. The singer supreme for half a century, she remained for her whole life in Sevilla, the city of her birth. She was gitana — a gypsy. Her way of singing los cantes gitanos — gypsy songs — was extremely personal. There were many who tried to imitate her but like Carmen Amaya in the dance and Manuel Torre in the male song she was inimitable. Her saetas during the Easter processions had a magical power and conviction. Her heyday came at the end of the

Pastora Pavón — La Niña de los Peines.

café cantante-epoch. Together with Chacón and Torre she maintained the greatness of the flamenco song during its incipient decadence. Picture on page 102.

Antonio Mairena, 1909–1983. In the foreword to a 1976 edition of Antonio Mairena's autobiography published in Sevilla, Ricardo Molina writes: "Antonio Mairena is the greatest singer of our time, comparable to the masters of the golden age of flamenco. I know no artist who, within his special field, has given more than what Mairena gave the song." In his book Mairena speaks of the problems of his art and gives exemplary advice to young singers, first and foremost to gypsies, his brothers in race and art. His personal thoughts about song are rooted in typical, century-old, race-centered gypsy debates, still unresolved. He was a great artist who had the ability, unusual for a gypsy, to conceive and formulate his own ideas about what was right and wrong in matters concerning his art. Picture on pages 54 and 64.

Manolo Caracol, 1909–1973, Madrid. He belonged to the large gypsy clan Ortega, with roots going back to El Planeta. His closest relatives were the most famous bull fighters and flamencos. He was of a wild and passionate nature and had no doubts whatsoever about his own greatness as a singer of cante gitano. There are many stories about his life and his life style: during his life he squandered large sums of money; he spent huge sums on big parties where he mixed members of the aristocracy with the highest paid

Manolo Caracol.

prostitutes, always insisting on paying the whole bill himself. Otherwise there was a row. He was a great singer when he wanted to but he could degenerate into singing simple, vulgar songs. His longstanding, extremely passionate relationship with **Lola Flores** is legendary. Seeing these two together on stage where he sang and she danced was thunder and lightning which

103

culminated in an exit number where anything could happen. Picture on page 103.

La Fernanda and **la Bernarda de Utrera**, 1923–, and 1926–, respectively. Two inseparable gypsy sisters from the song village Utrera near Sevilla. Fernanda is the most well known, but both belong to the highest class of cantaoras. An intimate atmosphere with an appreciative and understanding audience provides the best scope for their talents. They seldom sing in the tablaos. Picture on page 52.

Fosforito, Antonio Díaz, 1931–, Córdoba. Pict. on page 56.

José Menese, 1942–, Sevilla. Picture on page 54.

El Lebrijano.

El Lebrijano, 1941–, Lebrija. Picture on page 104.

José Mercé, 1955–, Jerez de la Frontera. Pict. on page 69.

These four young singers are among the modern celebrities within el cante, famous far outside their homeland. From their beginnings as singers in los tablaos, they have turned to solo engagements and singing in *festivales*. Festivales de flamenco are flamenco competitions organized in many of Spain's larger cities, Madrid, Barcelona, Valencia, Córdoba, Sevilla, Granada, Málaga, to name the most important, but also in smaller cities and villages around the country. There young singers, dancers and guitarists can present themselves and get a chance to go further, and established artists can demonstrate their art and go on to fame and glory. For an outsider this is a unique opportunity to listen to, look at and learn flamenco in order to understand more about this art.

Dancers

La Macarrona, Juana Vargas, 1860–1947. This magnificent bailaora belonged to the golden age of flamenco. She was famous for her sculptured beauty and for the dance where she handled the huge Manila shawl and her *bata de cola* — dress with a train — superbly. Maneuvering the train on a bata de cola skillfully and elegantly demands a great deal of practice and is an art in itself.

La Malena, 1870–1953. Who was the greatest — la Malena or la Macarrona? Both were brilliant artists — which of them one preferred was a question of taste. But there was no doubt that these two were the masters of the classical flamenco dance.

La Argentina, 1886–1936. Whatever is written about Antonia Mercé — La Argentina — is an understatement. She was the great, unsurpassed dance artist in Spain. Thanks to her talent, beauty, intelligence and creative power she was the one who rejuvenated the dance in Spain at a time when the art of flamenco was being downgraded and the classical bolero dance was dying out.

She was born in Buenos Aires, whence comes the artist name, of an Andalusian mother and a Castilian father. She was a mixture of the Andalusian grace, flexibility and musicality and the Castilian bearing and sense of style.

La Argentina.

She had a command of the various forms of the Spanish dance: the bolero school, folk dance and flamenco. She also renewed the castanet playing, allowing the castanet makers to experiment with various materials to vary the playing and elicit nuances in the tone. She created dances to the music of the young composers, such as Albeniz, Granados and de Falla. The Parisians loved her; she gave dance recitals there, both solo and often with Vicente Escudero, a great contemporary figure in the flamenco world. She made countless tours throughout the world. Fernando el de Triana wrote a panegyric to her, saying: "She is today — 1920's–1930's — the best bailarina in the universe; no one can question that." Unfortunately she died all too young of illness. Pictures on pages 95 and 106.

Vicente Escudero, born in Valladolid in 1885, died in Barcelona in 1980. He was a particularly strange and controversial figure within the world of flamenco; a very strong personality, a self-willed artist. He paid no attention to the strict rules regarding tempo and rhythm in the various flamenco dances. He wanted to dance freely and naturally, exactly as he felt at the moment. In that respect he was like the

Vicente Escudero.

gypsies. He was payo, but the gypsies who were flamenco artists were very careful to follow and maintain the tempo and style in the various songs and dances. There he was unlike them. The audiences liked him anyway for his duende and for his strong and genuine radiance, but in the world of flamenco he was considered *loco* — crazy, and was not accepted there. Over the years, however, he learned the rules and became widely known both at home and abroad. He was the first to create a dance from the Siguiryia song; previous to this it had been respected as a song, much too sacred to be danced. In his old age he drew and painted very personal, surrealistic figures of flamenco dancers. Picture on page 106.

La Argentinita, Encarnación López, 1900–1945. Still another bailarina-bailaora born in Buenos Aires. She came to Spain early in life and began her career with regional dances. Later in her life she changed to flamenco but never became a full fledged bailaora. She was, however, the one who succeeded in setting flamenco into the theatre. She staged a kind of flamenco-show — Las Calles de Cádiz — the streets of Cádiz — with the best artists. It is said to have been a perfect way to present flamenco in the theatre. She had her own dance ensemble and often toured abroad, mostly in North and South America. She also died too young of illness.

Pilar López, 1906–, a sister of la Argentinita and danced with her and her ensemble up to la Argentinita's death in 1945. Pilar López then formed her own dance ensemble with which she has toured in many countries. She is a first-rate choreographer who has created many interesting ballets, some with classical, some with flamenco motifs. One of her particular strengths has been the instruction of young male dancers. Her art and her ballets reached their high point when her bailaores were **Manolo Vargas, Roberto Ximénez, José Greco, Alejandro Vega**. Picture on page 97.

La Quica, Francisca González, 1905–1967, Sevilla-Madrid. La Quica was a maestra, both as a dancer and as a teacher. She was a fine bailaora with temperament and style who has been a model for many dancers of yesterday and today. She married **Frasquillo León**, who had a dance-academy in Sevilla. They had a daughter — **Mercedes León** — who continued in her parents'

La Quica.

profession. La Quica was both bailaora and bailarina. she danced the classical bolero dances with a charm and an exquisite personableness which is unforgettable. Her version of *El Olé de la Curra*, a famous bolero dance, is a masterpiece. During the final years of her life she lived in Madrid and devoted herself mostly to teaching. Picture on page 108.

Carmen Amaya, 1913–1963. She was an explosion, a volcanic eruption on the stage. Most often she dressed in traje corto — the flamenco suit for men — with high waisted, tight-fitting trousers and short, closefitting jacket. Her body was more male than

Carmen Amaya.

female and so was her dancing. Legs of steel, feet of iron which stamped through more then one floor. Privately she is said to have been rather calm and completely feminine. Her zapateado — footwork — in combination with her dancers' palmas — handclapping — was a deafening orgy of rhythms. She revolutionized the female flamenco dance with her wild turns and quick steps. The traditional classical, quiet dance for bailaoras with its powerful and grandiose arm movements and twisting of the upper body went out of fashion; all the young dancers tried to imitate Carmen — with poor results. Thank goodness the original style of bailaoras is on its way back. She died of a severe illness and flamenco dance lost a unique individual, a bailaora who will go down in history as one of the greats. Picture on page 109.

Antonio Ruiz Soler, 1921– and **Rosario**, 1914–, Sevilla. Antonio and his partner, Rosario, are probably the dance couple who have contributed most to making the Spanish dance, especially flamenco, known throughout the world. In Sevilla they began to study with maestro **Realito**, who had a famous académia de baile — dance school. There they were discovered while still very young. Antonio was not more than seven when he got his first professional engagement at the Teatro Duque in Sevilla. Although Antonio was the younger, he was the leading figure. He was careful to see to it that Rosario did not get in his way. He was also an exceptional dance talent who as an adult would eventually master absolutely all the forms of dance in Spain, including classical ballet.

As children and adolescents they studied with maestros like **Otero, Pericet** in bolero dance and with **Frasquillo** in flamenco.

Antonio and Rosario.

They were: called Los Chavalillos Sevillanos — The Children of Sevilla — and toured round the country at an early age. Then came great tours in South and North America and eventually in most of the countries of the world. By 1952 they had worked as a dance couple for twenty-two years. They went their separate ways then after many disagreements.

Antonio formed a large ballet company with ballets in both the traditional and innovative spirit. He conceived a ballet to de Falla's *Amor brujo* — Love, The Magician — which had its premiere in London at the Saville Theatre where he, according to the critics, penetrated the depths of de Falla's music, giving it life and spirit. But he was greatest as a dancer. He is admired and honoured by everyone, both audience and critics. He is a genius, a God of the dance.

As a dancer Rosario is inevitably linked to Antonio. She is a splendid dancer with superb artistic sense and dramatic insight, but she does not have Antonio's strong personality and radiance. She also formed her own ballet ensemble and continued her dance career after her separation from Antonio. Pictures on pages 65 and 110.

Rosa Durán, 1922–, Jerez de la Frontera. In the chapter "From Cafés Cantantes to the Present Day" there is a description and a tribute to Rosa Durán and her dance at the tablao Zambra. Picture on page 82.

Mariemma.

Mariemma, 1917–, Valladolid. Bailarina. Musical, quick, feminine, technically perfect without showing it off. Her castanet playing is superb, musical; she has mastered dances from all the regions of Spain and composes her own dances. Dancing to the guitar is also a number in her repertoire even if flamenco does not come naturally to her. An esteemed and high class artist. Picture on page 111.

Mercedes León, 1923–, Sevilla and Madrid. Daughter of La Quica and Frasquillo, the famous maestro of Sevilla who died much too soon. Educated at an early age in the technique and dances of the bolero school, she has as a resource all of the exercises, methods and repertoire of that school as well as the traditional classical flamenco's style and dances. All the regional dances and styles are also part of her expertise. Her dance partner, who also is her life partner, is **Albano de Zuñiga**, 1923–. Together they have toured South and North America and all of Europe, a unique spellbinding couple who for many years have had one of the finest schools of dance in Spain where many seek admittance. They have been invited to many countries as guest teachers. Picture on page 96.

Matilde Coral, 1935–, Sevilla. She is a bailaora of the highest and purest quality. In her youth she could be seen at los tablaos in Madrid, where her demonstrations of flamenco were superb. Her jondo dances have the slow, majestic characteristics which the classical female dance ought to have. Every second, every inch of her dance is full of concentration and a radiance which fills the entire hall. She is a great, genuine bailaora. Pictures on pages 63 and 88.

El Farruco, Antonio Montoya Flores, 1936–, Madrid. A short, dynamic bailaor who can show us what flamenco is when he wants to. He saunters on to the stage in a tablao, chats a bit with his guitarist, strikes some palmas, completely relaxed. Then he stops and rivets his eyes on the audience, who suddenly sit straight up. After a couple of seconds of immobility and dead silence he breaks loose with his feet like a machine gun and perhaps does a few vehement twirls. Then motionless again. The audience is breathless. El Farruco has primitive wildness in his dance which is absolutely genuine, not theatre. Pictures on page 63.

Antonio Gades and Carmen Mora.

Antonio Gades, 1938–. Born in Alicante, resident of Madrid. He belongs to the group of top artists within flamenco dance, both as a dancer and a choreographer. He became famous for his wonderful dance in the well known film *Los Tarantos*, with Carmen Amaya, among others. He danced for eight years with Pilar López's company and learned everything about classical, regional and flamenco dance. Afterwards he formed his own company with the finest female soloists, such as **Cristina Hoyos** among others. In recent years he has made several brilliant films with film director **Carlos Saura**: *Blood wedding* after García Lorca's play, *Carmen* after Bizet's opera, *El Amor Brujo* and several others. In these his choreography is very exciting, both restrained and imaginative. Blood Wedding in particular unites simplicity with a dramatic power seldom seen in filmed dance. Picture on page 113.

José de Udaeta, 1919–, Barcelona. He studied classical dance and flamenco dance with La Quica and was her partner for a time. He and **Susana Audeoud**, 1919–, Köniz, Switzerland toured as a couple for twenty years in many countries and continents. They also gave courses in all types of Spanish dance.

113

José de Udaeta.

They did their own choreography, often with well known Spanish motifs, such as Don Juan, La Celestina, Orfeo Gitano, etc. They engaged flamenco singers and guitarists for their flamenco-inspired ballets. After their years together on tour, they each went their separate ways. José teaches and gives courses mostly in Germany. For many years he has organized and led summer courses with excellent teachers in Sitges near Barcelona. The courses attract many students from European countries and even from countries far away. His head teachers there are Mercedes and Albano; see above. His specialty today is castanet playing, of which he is a master of perfection. Picture on page 114.

Cristina Hoyos, 1946–, Sevilla. A great talent, a great bailaora who began her career in Sevilla at the age of twelve. Best known as partner of Antonio Gades', she performs nowadays mainly with her own company. In the films, *Blood Wedding*, *Carmen* and *Amor Brujo* she gave fantastic performances of her

Enrique el Cojo teaching.

authentic jondo dance; she attracts a large audience. In Sevilla she participated in the flamenco festival in 1988, and when she made her entrance on stage the audience rose and shouted Reina, reina — queen, queen. In 1991 she was awarded the National Dance Price by the Spanish Ministry of Culture and also the Andalusian Gold Medal for Arts. Picture on pages 3 and 91.

Enrique el Cojo, Enrique the Lame, 1912–1986, Sevilla. A lame bailaor! It is difficult to imagine. As a child he contracted an illness which left him lame in one leg but despite his injury he became a great name within the art of flamenco. His love of the dance induced him to begin to study for Ángel Pericet and Frasquillo in Sevilla, where he lived. In his youth he associated with famous dancers. He won prizes in competitions and performed in El Kursaal in Sevilla, a café cantante which survived in spite of the decadence. Later he became famous as a teacher; many

El Güito and Manuela Vargas.

famous dancers have studied with him and been influenced by his style and proficiency. For a time he was engaged at the famous tablao in Madrid, El Corral de la Morería, a great event in Madrid's flamenco world. He also had his own tablao in Sevilla. His dance was pure and simple, with subtlety and charm. Despite his handicap and his corpulence as an older man, his dance was flamenco puro of the highest order. Picture on page 115.

Manuela Vargas, 1941–, Sevilla. Bailaora gitana, one of the most important artists of today, as a dancer and as a choreographer. While still very young she studied and cooperated with Enrique el Cojo in Sevilla. She has travelled and danced in many countries, creating a sensation everywhere for her pure, authentic, personal and dramatic style and radiance. Splendid words have been said and written about her; here is a quote from José María Pemán: "Manuela Vargas is a dark beauty; she is music, movement and rhythm. She has that nameless mystery which is elegance and style: She is the mistress of space, air and light." Picture on page 116.

La Tati, 1940–, Madrid. La Tati belongs to the elite of today's dancers. She was discovered by La Quica, who took her as a special pupil. She spent practically her whole childhood in La Quica's studio, where she was always present at the classes and surreptitiously learned all of Quica's dances. She began her career at Zambra where she was able to learn from Rosa Durán. Other tablaos followed, then various tours with stars like Paco de Luća (guitarist), El Lebrijano (singer) and others. Today she is known as a personable and versatile bailaora with a magnetic power in her dance which puts the audience in a state of excitement. She sometimes tours with her own group of two male dancers plus singers and musicians. Picture on page 60.

Blanca del Rey, 1949, Córdoba. See page 98. Picture on page 140.

In Spain today there are many other gifted dancers who deserve to be mentioned. A list follows below:

El Güito, 1942–, Madrid. Picture on pages 92 and 116.

Merche Esmeralda, 1952–, Sevilla.

Javier Barón, 1963–, Sevilla.

Manolete, 1945–, Granada.

Antonio Canales, 1962–, Sevilla.

Guitarists

As mentioned earlier the guitar became a part of the art of flamenco rather late. For several hundred years there was only song and dance, closely enclosed within the gypsy clan or in small taverns. During the first primitive epoch of flamenco, 1800–1860, guitar playing began to exist as an accompaniment. Virtuoso solo playing emerged during the café cantanteperiod.

Habichuela, 1860–1927, Cádiz, is considered to be the first really skillful accompanist for both song and dance. He often played for Antonio Chacón and was La Niña de los Peines' special accompanist. There are nine flamenco artists of the same name besides the one named here, seven of them guitarists, one bailaora, one cantaora. Some of them are from the same family.

Javier Molina, 1868–1956, Jerez. He played with inspiration and duende to the older and more difficult songs and dances and was constantly in demand as an accompanist. Fernando El de Triana paid tribute to him with the words: "Javier Molina is the guitarist who is most anxious to preserve the accompaniments to the old songs, but he is without doubt an 'atom' (= a zero) when the singer gets going."

Ramón Montoya, 1880–1949. Gypsy. Is most famous for his innovations within guitar playing: a virtuoso soloist who created a new style in guitar playing. He has been called the father of the modern playing style and will go down in history as a great creative artist. In his Encyclopedia, which contains everything about flamenco, José Blas Vega mentions twentyfour flamenco artists named Montoya.

Manolo de Huelva, 1892–1976, Sevilla. He also belongs to the circle of innovators and was a strong and creative player with duende.

Perico el del Lunar — Perico with the Birthmark, 1894–1964, Jerez. He played the guitar all his life. A matchless accompanist for the great singers and dancers of his time. He could and did accompany all the songs, both the old and new; less well known was his predilection for dance. He knew the entire repertoire and for a long while was the inspiration for Rosa Durán's brilliant dancing.

Manolo de Badajoz, 1892–1962 and his son **Justo de Bada-**

joz, 1927–, both from Badajoz. Manolo was one of the most distinguished accompanists to el cante. His son Justo plays a more modern flamenco than his father, influenced by classical playing. He is a fine soloist. Picture on page 69.

Sabicas, 1913–, Pamplona. When he was seven years old he made his debut as a soloist in his home city. As a ten year old boy he came to Madrid where he continued his career. He became famous and was constantly honoured for the imagination and innovation of his playing, which left important traces in the development of guitar playing. There are several reasons for the greatness of this guitarist. He has an incredible technique, a superb sense of tempo and a special gift for accompaniment. He was Carmen Amaya's favourite guitarist.

Melchor de Marchena, 1908–1980, Marchena. When this guitarist was asked what he considered the most essential element in flamenco playing, he answered: "To play from the soul." This usually applies to all great art, but at the same time when Melchor de Marchena was greatest, flamenco abounded with technically oriented, superficial players. Melchor was flamenco puro and played the primitive jondo music with feeling and insight. He accompanied Manolo Caracol on his tours in Europe and America and made many gramophone records with Caracol and Antonio Mairena.

Luis Maravilla, 1914–, Sevilla. One of flamenco's most eminent guitarists, especially as an accompanist. He has won many prizes in guitar competitions. He has played for most of the

Paco de Lucía.

119

famous singers and dancers of his time and for a long period belonged to Pilar López' dance company. Maravilla also studied classical guitar but his first love was flamenco, whose stimulus and duende were vital to him.

Paco de Lucía, 1947–, Algeciras. Paco de Lucía is a revolutionary. He was brought up and educated by his father, who early discovered his son's talent and aptitude for the guitar playing. As a teenager he won prizes in many competitions in different parts of the country. He received his real foundation in flamenco from his father and became a fine accompanist. Authentic flamenco was important to him, but his facility for technique and his need to progress, to do something new, and his constant inner restlessness drove him to search out new paths. He became fascinated by other musical forms such as Brazilian music; bossa nova, rumba, samba. The rhythms and sounds became part of his playing, as well as jazz and other black music. He received a certain amount of criticism for this within his own country, but for the young musicians ha became an idol, a revolutionary. One speaks of playing before and after Paco de Lucía. As a guitarist he resembles no one else. he admires and respects traditional greatness at the same time that he has an irrepressible need to do something different, even though that desire sometimes leads him on to strange paths. His playing is completely effortless, technically perfect, authentic all the way through and he has great creative power. Picture on page 119.

Enrique de Melchor, 1951–. Son of Melchor de Marchena. An excellent guitarist, belonging to the best of today. Just as good an accompanist as virtuoso soloist with his own compositions. Picture on page 70.

This is a small selection from the large group of eminent guitarists, the earlier ones as well as the younger ones of today. If any reader wishes to study the subject more deeply and learn more about flamenco guitarists and guitar playing, the chapter "The guitar" in Lives and Legends of Flamenco published by D.E Pohren, Madrid, 1988, can be recommended. For those who read Spanish, La Guitarra by Manuel Cano, Córdoba, 1986, is an excellent book, full of information about the history of the guitar and its role in the art of flamenco. The book also contains two cassettes.

SOME MAJOR FESTIVALS

The April Festival in Sevilla

Sevilla, the praised city in southwest Andalusia, surrounded by wide fields of grain, meadows and olive groves, with the Sierra Morena in the background and the shimmering river Guadalquivir cutting through it, is the scene of this delightful, happy festival.

But before we dance into the festival, a little prologue about Sevilla.

The festival is preceded by the *Semana Santa,* — the Holy Week — Easterweek. In every city and village on the Iberian peninsula religious processions, rituals and other events take place during Eastertide, as in all catholic countries, but Sevilla's Easter celebration takes the prize for combining external splendour with living, inner perception. Day and night the richly ornamented holy images of the saints are carried around the city on their catafalques, all of them passing through the cathedral. Innumerable members of the various brotherhoods, dressed in their capes and high conical hats with holes for the eyes, walk barefoot in front and behind. The entire population participates in this enormous exhibition of faith and worship. As an outsider, suddenly plunged into these events, one is overwhelmed, questioning, fascinated or frightened.

After these intensive days and nights in the world of the spirit the Sevillians need a little interval of calm and relaxation. But after only a few days they begin to prepare for the festival.

Feria means fair. The Sevilla Fair in April was originally a horse and cattle fair. People gathered from near and far at the fair on the outskirts of the city to do business with their horses, donkeys, mules and cattle in general. Country folk and city folk, old and young, even children went there to meet each other, do business, eat and drink, sing and dance, to "paint the town red."

This fair was founded in 1847 by a few families from the Sevillian aristocracy and since then has grown in importance and popularity. The horse trading is gone now; what remains is an enormous, fantastic popular festival, corteges and horsemen, equipages, dance, song, wine and beautiful clothing. And bull fighting, of course.

The festival is primarily for Sevillians but hither people come from near and far, from the whole country and from other nations. All the hotels are full, every private room rented out; there is not a bed to be had during this week. Rooms must be reserved far in advance if one doesn't have an acquaintance or a relative in the city. Homes are filled to the bursting point by cousins and aunts and uncles from other cities.

Up until about 1970 the festivities took place in a park on the eastern outskirts of the city but the festival grew and it had to be moved to a larger area south of the river. Today hundreds of small tent-like houses, *casetas* — little house — are situated along broad avenues of acacia trees there. The casetas are open to the street and have an outer room where people can sit or dance, sing and play the guitar and a dark inner room where all the refreshments, wine and soft drinks can be found and where the Sevillian *tapas* (snacks served with the wine) are prepared. The houses are made of a simple iron scaffolding over which striped canvas fabric is stretched and they always have wooden floors to dance on. Paper roses and garlands decorate the ceiling and the walls; ornamental lamps shine at night.

Hundreds of riders take part in the Parade.

These casetas are private; they are owned by families or societies and clubs, banks and businesses. Every public institution has its caseta and only those who belong to the family, society, institution, etc. and their friends are allowed to enter the casetas. An outsider can not come into a caseta unless he has been specially invited. But there are open restaurants and bars for strolling tourists and strangers. There is often a low stage in the center where professional artists perform and which is open to all who can and wish to dance sevillanas. And almost everyone can and wish to. Children, old folks and young people.

From innumerable loudspeakers pour the sounds of sevillanas, fandangos, malagueñas, paso-dobles — but mostly sevillanas. Song, guitar playing, the rhythms of castanets, palmas and zapateados can be heard through the whole district.

The most striking and fascinating aspect of the festival and typical of the whole, is the activity surrounding horses. This is a remnant of the old fair which has left commerce behind and now only displays the beauty, power and elegance of the Andalusian breed of horses.

At noon when the sun is high in the sky the parading, *el paseo* — the promenade — begins. Along the broad streets with ten rows of Chinese lanterns come the decorated and bejewelled horses with their proud, arrogant riders. Their girls sit *a la grupa* — on the horses' loins — behind the rider and spread out their colourful frilled skirts over the horses' hind quarters and tail.

Wagons hitched to two, four or six horses are drawn slowly and magnificently along the streets. The drivers, like the horse-men, are dressed in the traditional Andalusian riding habit, *traje campero*, tight fitting trousers, boots, short jackets and Cordoban hats. Beautiful women together with children and older men often sit in the wagons. Against the back support at the rear of the carriage sit young girls in the traditional *traje gitana* — gypsy dress — with polka dots and frills. The dresses float out over the rear of the carriage and they sit there like queens to be admired, arms akimbo in the Spanish posture. And admired they are by all the strollers who crowd at the sides between las casetas and the horse parade. Olés and other typical exclamations of appreciation

A quiet interval by the casetas.

124

and delight — *piropos* — are heard everywhere. The tramp of horses' feet, the murmur of the people in party mood and the music from the loudspeakers blend in a resounding symphony of sound. Horse and rider are of the greatest importance in Sevillian life. According to Ortega y Gasset tradition and culture in Andalucía la Baja — lower Andalusia — is the epitome of a peaceful agricultural peasant society in contrast to the stern, warlike character of that in Castile. Riding and "knowing" horses are for the Andalusian a need, an absolute necessity, an ancient cult belonging in part to the work of the farm, in part to hunting and other equine sports. Rounding up bulls demands great skill and assurance in the saddle, not to mention fighting and killing a bull from the back of a galloping horse.

At the festival in Sevilla el paseo, the parade with horses, riders and the magnificent equipages with all their splendid accessories, is the great spectacle one admires, applauds and is proud of.

The harnesses are hung with small red balls in tufted bouquets and bells which jingle rhythmically to the horses' steps. Manes and tails are often skillfully braided. The horseman, with or without girl behind him, rides slowly along the streets, conscious of glances from everyone. Now and then he stops and joins a little group to have a glass of *vino fino* — light, dry sherry — and a chat.

For that matter anyone can rent a carriage for an hour or two to ride around and feel *with* and *in* the whole thing.

While the paseo goes on people sit in their casetas, drink wine, talk, laugh and enjoy each others' company immensely. They visit each other, invite friends and acquaintances, argue and gossip: *did* you see her dress, why is *she* sitting on *his* horse etc. They dance a round of sevillanas when the fancy strikes them.

On the streets people walk back and forth as the corteges pass; social relations are just as lively there as in las casetas. Some are dressed in their ordinary finery, but most of the women of all ages wear splendid flowing Sevillian dresses in every conceivable colour and pattern. The little girls resemble fantastic flowers, swaying and bending, and the boys of the same age are dressed

The girls ride "a la grupa" in their colourful skirts.

from head to toe in Andalusian *traje corto* — high waisted trousers, white shirts and short jackets, Cordoban hats.

At the far end of the area there is a completely equipped amusement park with carousels, swings, radio cars and everything a child could wish for and this, of course, attracts children and their parents. There is a fearful racket, screams. laughter and high decibel loudspeaker music but this part can be avoided.

These events occur in the forenoon beginning at about eleven o'clock. At about two or three most of the activity comes to a standstill. It is time for lunch and siesta. *La comida* is the best meal of the day. Then one eats well, sitting at table for a long time. Andalusia may not have the best cuisine in the country (it is the Basque, Galician and Catalonian in the North which have that) but shell-fish and goat dishes are excellent. *Huevos a la flamenca*, fried egg with *chorizo* — strongly spiced sausage — and vegetables is a standing first course and *gazpacho*, the cold soup made of raw vegetables with bread, olive oil and lots of garlic, is a delicious dish in the heat. Full of bread and spectacle, everyone then goes to his siesta in order to be able participate in the coming night's festivities with renewed strength.

When darkness falls the whole festival explodes in a sea of light. Garlands of thousands of coloured bulbs light up the streets and the casetas. The huge entry bridge with its two towers is like a cascade of fire. People move easily, livelier than during the day and now the dance begins, sevillanas, in earnest. Everywhere in the casetas, in the restaurants, on the streets, the dance is in full swing to the rhythm of song, guitar, castanet and palmas. Grown-ups and children dance with each other: mothers with little sons, fathers with little daughters, boys with girls, older folks with younger. If one is a foreigner and can dance sevillanas, this is an added attraction and one is invited everywhere.

On the streets small, tight rings of people form. They sing and clap for one or several couples dancing in the center. Everything is in motion, vibrating with music and rhythm, shouts and laughter. Few are drunk but now and then a few staggering young boys can be seen who, laughing uncontrollably, try to dance a sevillana with each other. The final pose is often a sitting position on the street.

In many casetas professional dancers and singers are

engaged. The passionate and provocative tones and rhythms of light flamencos, bulerías and rumba flamenca pour out.

Gradually, toward the small hours, the tempo and activity moderate; many go home. The young people stay as long as they can, strolling about in groups, trying to keep the intoxication going, but everything ends at last. Las casetas and the restaurants close, the lights are turned off and the whole area is in darkness, resting a few hours until the next morning when everything will begin again from the beginning. But first it is cleaned, swept and rinsed by efficient communal street cleaners in smart uniforms.

Everything which has been described so far applies to the festival area, the scene of the festivities. But life inside the city is also marked by the festival. A steady stream of festively dressed people pours through the streets and flows over the bridges in the direction of the festival. With hasty steps, expectation in their glances, talking and singing, they go to the festival in the forenoon. At night they walk homeward, exhausted, with dawdling footsteps. The city blossoms with polka dotted, frilled dresses, hats, shawls, fans. It hums with sound and rhythms. In the narrow streets of Barrio de Santa Cruz palmas and castanets echo by night and sevillanas is danced round the clock.

Not only dancing and horses are in evidence during the week the festival lasts. There are also bulls. Bullfights are an integral part of all folk festivals in Spain. Every day. *A las cinco de la tarde* — at five o'clock in the afternoon.

La Maestranza, the most beautiful *plaza de toros* — bullfight arena — in the country, is filled every afternoon during the festival by a merry, boisterous, expectant audience. The best, most famous, highest paid matadors are engaged. Promptly at the stroke of five or six when everyone has taken his seat, the doors are opened and *el paseo*, the splendid opening ceremony, begins. They say that this is the only occasion when Spaniards are exactly on time.

The sunshine on the golden sand is blinding. La Maestranza is a wide, low arena where late in the afternoon the shadows creep up toward the center. The classically well proportioned arcades, however, provide shade for the spectators highest up in the galleries. Either *Sol* or *sombra* — sun or shade: whether the seat is in the sun or shade decides the ticket price. People of all sorts go to bullfights. They are of all ages, come from all classes high and low, rich and poor and everything in between. People who can pay the extremely high ticket prices sit in the shade. Among them are aristocrats with beautiful ladies who spread out their *mantones de Manila* — large, embroidered silk shawls from Manila — on *la barrera* — the barrier in front of the the best seats closest to the arena. Here sit many *aficionados* — the real enthusiasts, many with season tickets for their seats. In the final period of the bullfight during the infighting with the *muleta* — red cloth — and before the actual slaying, the matador often steers the bull to this part of the arena.

The seats in the sun are considerably cheaper, but many aficionados sit there as well, plus throngs of all kinds of people. Some bull fighters with a sense of justice or a desire to gain popularity take their bulls out into the sun towards these spectators and they are then greeted by enormous ovations.

A medium priced ticket is available for places in *Sol y sombra* — sun and shade — where the sun is hot and blinding only in the beginning but then disappears.

When the fight is over, usually after six bulls have been killed, the spectators walk slowly out. The frenzy is over; the narrow exit aisles are crowded; most people head for the bars and cafés for a glass of wine or beer or a cup of coffee and long discussions about every detail of the bullfight.

Daily life continues as usual during this festival week. Many take holiday, but most workers carry on with their jobs as best they can, hurrying out to the festival in the evening. Late nights and early mornings for seven days are the lot of many.

La Romería del Rocío — An incomparable folk festival

La Virgen del Rocío — the Virgin of Rocío — is the main character in this incomparable folk festival. After her come the horses, hundreds of horses of the Andalusian race, powerful, well-built, with short, strong necks; proud, beautiful carriage; long manes and tails; alert eyes and ears; lively and confident. Then the people, ordinary people: thirty or forty thousand of them gather in el Rocío every year.

El Rocío is a little place in Andalusia in southwest Spain about midway between the cities of Huelva and Cádiz. It is situated in las Marismas, a rather desolate part of the country, a flat marshland near the Atlantic, a nature preserve with birds, horses and bulls.

This incredible folk festival takes place during Whitsuntide every year.

Legend says that one day about 400 years ago a hunter from Almonte, a little village north of el Rocío, was out hunting. His dogs paused at a thicket but there was no quarry. He searched the thicket and found in a hollow tree there an image of the Blessed Virgin. He took her with him, intending to bring her back to Almonte. The heavy burden tired him and he lay down to sleep. When he awoke the Virgin had disappeared. He went back to the hollow tree and there was the Virgin again. He left her and went home to tell about the miracle. Some of the villagers who doubted his story walked the long distance back to the place he described and found the Virgin in the tree. They tried to carry her to Almonte but again she disappeared and returned to her tree. The men then related the event to the village priest who explained that this meant that the Virgin wished to show them her desire to be worshiped there. After this they built a chapel for her on the site where the tree stood and named her "Nuestra Señora del Rocío" — The Virgin of Rocío — after the place, La Rocina, where she had been found.

Since that time El Rocío has become a shrine and every year at Whitsun tens of thousands of people make pilgrimages to it.

Hermandades — brotherhoods — come by wagon and on horseback, not only from every district and village in the vicinity, but also from Sevilla, Córdoba, Granada, Jerez and even from Madrid and other distant places.

The journey to Rocío is in itself a great part of the enjoyment of the festival. They travel in *carretas* — wagons with arched roofs made of sturdy cloth, like covered wagons, drawn by oxen or mules. Inside can be found everything which is required for the journey and for the three days and nights which the festival lasts; mattresses, blankets, pillows, clothing, household utensils, para-

Next page: On the way to Rocío.

131

ffin stoves, food, wine etc. Underneath the wagons hang cages of fresh food, such as living hens, chickens and rabbits. Every brotherhood may have up to ten wagons in which the women and children ride. Men and even many women travel on horseback. They sleep in the wagons and outdoors on the ground during the trip.

La Capila — the Chapel — the shrine where *La Virgen* is displayed at the altar, is the center and focal point. In a half circle a little in front of her is a high wrought iron railing where people cling to kneel and pray. In the whole white, clean chapel there is a constant movement of people going in and out or standing still in prayer and worship. It is very crowded but there is never any sign of impatience or irritation.

El Rocío is situated among sand dunes and pine woods and the ground is of sand. One walks, rides and drives on sand. Everyone has sturdy boots, even the women under their long, wide polka dotted, frilled dresses.

Behind the chapel is the large central square *El Real del Rocío* along the sides of which there are low, white houses with covered, narrow verandas. Many brotherhoods have these at their disposal to receive friends and acquaintances, drink wine, eat tapas, olives, sausages, bread, cheese etc. and to sing, dance and just be together. Behind El Real all the wagons are parked and on the periphery are all the hundreds of tents where most people live. Only the brotherhoods from the largest and richest communities can afford their own *caseta* — house — on El Real and the surrounding streets.

On the Friday evening before Whitsun Eve the wagons have already begun to arrive and they continue to come all night long and all day Saturday. By Saturday noon the festival is in full swing. Booths have been set up to display jewelry, holy pictures, ceramics and quantities of nuts, dates, figs, candy and sweet specialties from the surrounding district. A few cafés and small restaurants serve chicken, sausages, cheese and the famous *jamón jabugo*, a lightly smoked and salted ham which tastes divine but is very expensive. Vino fino — dry sherry — and ordinary wine can be found everywhere, of course. The eating places are simple,

The men fight for a place to carry La Virgen.

even primitive — lots of plastic and tin plate and other cheap material — but what one gets to eat and drink is first class.

At 12 o'clock on Saturday the brotherhoods begin to gather at El Real for the first procession around the chapel and La Virgen. Farthest forward is the wagon with the brotherhood's own emblem, *El Simpecado*, drawn by oxen or mules. Simpecado means, literally translated, without sin — the blameless — the righteous. El Simpecado is the name of the emblem which carries the picture of La Virgen either on a banner, richly adorned with embroidery in silver and gold, or on a large tablet embossed in silver and gold. The wagon has two large, white, spoked wheels almost two meters in diameter, a superstructure of six ornamented silver posts supporting a roof of silver, candelabra of silver and candles with bell-glass and masses of flowers over the whole. Even the oxen and mules are adorned with painted and decorated yokes, tufts and bells. Behind El Simpecado come las carretas, the covered wagons, with women and children, the women and little children dressed in their polka dotted dresses, fringed shawls, large earrings, with flowers in their hair. In front, behind, all around ride the men and boys. Last come those on foot. Every brotherhood's procession stops in front of the chapel and "La Salve", a blessing is sung. This goes on for hours until late in the afternoon when everyone gradually goes home to eat, drink and take a well earned siesta.

There is constant motion among horses and riders at the same time as the procession is taking place. Back and forth on El Real and on the streets alongside the houses the horses and the riders show off in all their glory, walking, trotting, galloping or running at top speed. Horsemen of all ages dressed in all manner of styles, from the elegant caballero in short jacket, pin striped trousers turned up over his boots and *sahones* — a protective leather piece (like chaps) worn over legs and hips and decorated with metal buttons or other ornaments — to the hippie figure with long, tangled hair, dressed in jeans and a dirty shirt. They all ride "like Gods", welded to the saddle, at one with the horses, an incredible posture, relaxed, with the left hand holding the reins, the right hand on the hip. Some of them show off, letting the

Viva La Blanca Paloma!

horse prance rear, whirl around and do other tricks. Most of them ride in saddles with supports at the back and front and wide stirrups with support for the whole foot, but others, especially the jeans clad youths, ride bareback. Sometimes whole groups come tearing through the pedestrians but no one takes offense. On the contrary they laugh and admire them even though they know you can get a horse "kiss" if you don't watch out.

On Saturday evening the festival bursts out again, now in earnest. All the people and animals are in action, making an incredible din, screaming and laughing, singing and dancing, banging and playing. To *palmas y tambor* — handclapping and drums — they sing and dance wherever there is room — inside las casetas, outside on the verandas, on the sand of El Real and on the streets. It is Sevillanas and Sevillanas which are sung and danced during the Rocío festival. The melodies and the lyrics are old or new, happy and a bit risqué, or a little melancholy and romantic. Every year new lyrics and melodies appear but the dances, the old couple dances from Sevilla, are always the same. These are really genuine folk dances which everyone joins in, all ages from three to seventy. Groups are formed everywhere or rings with couples dancing in the center, spectators clapping and shouting along, some singing and drumming. Four Sevillanas are danced in every round, then one changes partners and begins all over again. The girls dance gently, are really feminine, the boys are more austere; their arms waving high over their heads. Everyone begins, changes sides and stops at exactly the same time. Everywhere above the crowds one sees these swaying arms flying in the air. There is speed, whirling and heat in the dance.

As the sound and movement increases in intensity, the horsemen begin to gallop wildly through the streets and among the people and a few collisions here and there can not be avoided. The riding, the dance, the song, the drums, the mad crowds; the crazy mood goes on all night.

On Sunday morning the atmosphere is completely different. There is a Mass at 10 o'clock out on El Real before the altar, moved there for the service. It is an extraordinary experience to see all the riders dismount and kneel while the horses stand absolutely still nearby.

Later on Sunday the festival continues, perhaps somewhat

more muted and less crowded (one has to sleep sometime), but in the evening it is in progress again, culminating in a glorious fireworks display.

On Monday something new occurs. Early in the morning La Virgen is lifted down from her place in the shrine and placed on a catafalque to be carried round to bless all the pilgrims who have come in her honour.

The tradition is that the men from Almonte who found her shall carry her but since others are allowed to try to take over the sacred burden, quarrels and fist fights brake out. Often she is on the verge of falling down but she is always rescued at the last minute. Rocking and shaking, she is carried slowly around for hours to the cheers and shouts, the noise and commotion of the crowd. They shout "Viva la blanca paloma" — long live the white dove — viva, viva, viva ...

After many hours she is finally brought back to her quiet place behind the iron railing in the chapel. The inflamed mood fades and most people seek out their beds. In the afternoon the wagons begin to roll homeward; tents, booths and cafés are dismantled; las casetas are closed. El Rocío regains its sublime calm after the wild, dramatic, incomparable festival and slumbers in its Sleeping Beauty sleep until the following Whitsuntide.

On the way back from Rocío. Drawing by Gustave Doré.

SUMMARY

There is naturally very much more to write and tell about flamenco. So many events, destinies, tragedies, jests and jokes and great occasions, so many details which go into the life of a gypsy can not be described in *one* book.

This book, FLAMENCO, deals with the historical background, with all the various immigrations to Spain, with the time when the troubled gypsy people began to move far away to the east in order to escape their persecutors, with their routes westward. It tells of their meeting with Spain, Andalusia and its people, of persecution and harassment and how song began to ease their difficult lives, the new striking, unknown songs which gradually broke free from the isolation of the gypsies; of how people became more and more aware of the fact that something new and exiting was happening here which must emerge. Then follows the epoch of cafés cantantes which had as a result that the song, the dance and the guitar playing, the art of flamenco, became known and renowned, first in Spain, and later in the world around. It reached South and North America, South Africa and naturally the rest of Europe, chiefly Paris and London, then eastward where Japan for a long time has shown keen

Blanca del Rey.

141

interest in and feeling for, one can say a passion for, flamenco in all its forms.

After the end of the second World War, when tourism began on a large scale, a constantly increasing number of people travelled to Spain where most of them encountered flamenco in some form.

During the 1950's the first signs of an active interest for flamenco awoke in several countries in Europe. Spanish dance groups begun touring England, Germany, France and the Scandinavian countries. An interest for Spanish dance and music begun to spread, young dancers and guitarists were enticed to go to Spain to see, listen and study. They came not only from Europe, but from South and North America, South Africa and especially from Japan where the art of flamenco had a quite remarkable response.

They returned to their respective homelands and shared their knowledge with their colleagues and since then interest and activities have continuously grown. Spanish dance began to be included in the curricula of most of the large schools of dance. Many people began to find great pleasure and relaxation in what was, for them, a new dance form, so rhythmic, flexible and stimulating.

Several young dance students showed great talent for the very special style and feeling in the Spanish dance. Today many competent dance teachers work with instruction in flamenco dance, classical Spanish dance and Spanish folk dance. Interest and knowledge are being spread in ever widening circles. Peñas flamencas — associations of flamenco enthusiasts — have arisen; societies and clubs arrange courses and presentations. Professional dance groups with flamenco programs have also been formed.

Flamenco has come to stay as a new art form with song, dance and guitar playing.

BIBLIOGRAPHY

Abbou, Is D: Musulmans Andalous et Judéo-Espagnols. Editions Antar, Casablanca 1953.

Alcalá, Miguel; Perez Orozco, Alfonso Eduardo: Le Flamenco et les Gitans. Editions Filipacchi, Paris 1987.

Almendros, Carlos: Todo lo básico sobre el flamenco. Ediciones Mundibro, Barcelona 1973.

Alvarez Caballero, Angel: Gitanos, Payos y Flamencos, en los Orígenes del Flamenco. Cinterco, Madrid 1988.

Arribas, Antonio: Los Iberos. Ayma S A Editora, Barcelona 1965.

Blas Vega, José: Los Cafés Cantantes de Sevilla. Editorial Cinterco, Madrid 1987.

Blas Vega, José; Ríos Ruiz, Manuel: Diccionario Enciclopédico Ilustrado del Flamenco, Part I and II. Editorial Cinterco, Madrid 1988.

Borrow, George: The Zincali or an Account of the Gypsies of Spain. John Murray, London 1843.

Caballero Bonald, José Manuel: El baile andaluz. Editorial Noguer, Barcelona 1967.

– Luces y sombras del flamenco. Al-Gaida Editores, Sevilla 1988.

Cano, Manuel: La Guitarra. Historia, Estudios y Aportaciones al Arte Flamenco. Ediciones Anel, Granada 1986.

Cansinos Assens, Rafael: La Copla Andaluza. Ediciones Demófilo, Madrid 1976.

Castejón, Rafael: Medina Azahara, third edition. Editorial Everest, León 1985.

Cervantes: Novelas Ejemplares. Nelson Editores, Paris 1951.

Chase, Gilbert: The Music of Spain. Dover Publications, New York 1959.

Davillier–Doré: Viaje por España (1862). Ediciones Castilla, Madrid 1957.

Ehrenpreis, Marcus: Landet mellan öster och väster. Hugo Gebers Förlag, Stockholm 1927.

Escudero, Vicente: Mi baile. Montaner y Simon, S A, Barcelona 1947.

Esquivel, Juan de: Arte del danzado. Facsimile edition 1947 of the original edition printed in Sevilla 1642 by Juan Gómes de Blas.

Estébanez Calderón, Serafín: La Andalucía de Estébanez, Antología. Tauros Ediciones, Madrid 1964.

Ford, Richard: Gatherings from Spain. J M Dent & Co, London 1906.

García Lorca, Federico: Obras completas. Third edition. Editorial Aguilar, Madrid 1957.

García Matos, Manuel: Castilla la Nueva. Sección Femenina de F E T, Madrid 1957.

– Extremadura. Sección Femenina de F E T, Madrid 1964.

– Andalucía. Sección Femenina del Movimiento, Madrid 1971.

– Sobre El Flamenco, Estudios y Notas. Editorial Cinterco, Madrid 1987.

García Ulecia, Alberto: Las Confesiones de Antonio Mairena. Publicaciones de la Universidad de Sevilla, Sevilla 1976.

Gómez-Tabanera, José M: Tesoro del folklore Español, Part I. Editorial Tesoro, Madrid 1950.

González Climent, Anselmo: Andalucía en los Toros, el Cante y la Danza. Sanchez Leal, Madrid 1953.

– Antología de Poesía Flamenca. Escelicer, Madrid 1961.

Grande, Félix: Memoria del Flamenco, Part I and II. Espasa-Calpe, S A, Madrid 1987.

Irving, Washington: Leyendas de la Conquista de España – Crónicas moriscas (translation from English). Miguel Sánchez, Editor, Granada 1974.

Ivanova, Anna: The dancing Spaniards. John Baker (Publishers), London 1970.

Lalagia: Spanish Dancing. Dance Books Ltd, London 1985.

Lafuente, Rafael: Los gitanos, el flamenco y los flamencos. Editorial Barna, Barcelona 1955.

Larrea, Arcadio: El Flamenco en su raíz. Editora Nacional, Madrid 1974.

– Guía del Flamenco. Editora Nacional, 1975.

Levinson, André: La Argentina. Editions des Chroniques du Jour. Paris 1928.

Manfredi Cano, Domingo: Geografía del cante jondo.

– Cante y baile flamencos. Editorial Everest, León 1973.

Marrero Suárez, Vicente: El acierto de la danza Española. Editorial Calamo, Madrid 1952.

Martinez de la Peña, Teresa: Teoría y práctica del baile flamenco. Aguilar S A de Ediciones, Madrid 1969.

Meri, La: Spanish Dancing. A S Barnes & Company, New York 1948.

– Spanish Dancing. The Eagle Printing and Binding Company, Pittsfield, Mass 1967.

Molina, Ricardo: Misterios del arte flamenco. Sagitario S A de Editores, Barcelona 1967.

Molina, Ricardo; Mairena, Antonio: Mundo y formas del cante flamenco. Librería Al-Andalus, Sevilla 1971.

Molina Fajardo, Eduardo: El flamenco en Granada. Miguel Sánchez, Editor, Granada 1974.

Monleón, José: Lo que sabemos del Flamenco. Gregório del Toro, Editor, Madrid 1967.

Niles, Doris: El Duende. Dance Perspectives, Inc, New York 1966.

Nuñes de Prado, Guillermo: Cantaores Andaluzes. Editoriales Andaluzas Unidas, Sevilla 1986.

Ortiz Muñoz, Luis: Sevilla Eterna. Editorial Seix Barral, Barcelona 1978.

Ortiz Nuevo, José Luis: De las Danzas y Andanzas de Enrique el Cojo. Portada Editorial, Sevilla 1984.

– Las Mil y Una Historias de Pericón de Cádiz. Ediciones Demófilo, Madrid 1975.

Otero, José: Tratado de bailes. Tipografia de la Guía Oficial, 1912.

Pemartín, Julián: El cante flamenco. Guía alfabética. Afrodisio Aguado, Madrid 1966.

Pohren, Donn E: Lives and Legends of Flamenco. Society of Spanish Studies, Madrid 1988.

– The art of flamenco. Dritte Auflage. Society of Spanish Studies, Madrid 1972.

– A Way of Life. Society of Spanish Studies, Madrid 1980.

Preciado, Dionisio: Folklore Español. Música, Danza y Ballet. Stvdium Ediciones, Madrid 1969.

Puig, Alfonso: Ballet y Baile Español. Montaner y Simon, Barcelona 1944.

– El arte del Baile Flamenco. Ediciones Polígrafa, Barcelona 1977.

Rodríguez Marín, Francisco: El alma de Andalucía. Revista de Archivos, Bibliotecas y Museos, Madrid 1929.

Rossy, Hipólito: Teoría del cante jondo. Credsa, Barcelona 1966.

Sachs, Curt: Eine Weltgeschichte des Tanzes. Dietrich Riemer/Ernst Wohsen, Berlin 1933.

145

Sanz de Pedre, Mariano: El pasodoble Español. Imp de José Luis Cosano, Madrid 1961.

Triana, Fernando el de: Arte y artistas flamencos. Second edition. Clan, Madrid 1952.

Udaeta, José de: Die Spanische Kastagnette, Ursprung und Entwicklung. Ulrich Steiner Verlag, Overath bei Köln 1985.

Vallecillo, Francisco: Antonio Mariena. Fundación Andaluza de Flamenco, Jerez 1988.

Watt, Montgomery: Historia de la España islámica (translation from English). Alianza Editorial, Madrid 1970.

✣

El Folklore Andaluz. Revista de Cultura Tradicional. 2.ª época, nr 1 and 2. Fundación Machado, Sevilla 1987.

El Folk-Lore Frexnense y Bético-Extremeño. Facsimile edition by Diputación Provincial de Badajoz and Fundación Antonio Machado, Sevilla 1988.

Folklore y Costumbres de España. Part I, II and III. Editorial Alberto Martin, Barcelona 1943–1946.

GLOSSARY

A

academia de baile	dance academy, dance school
aficionado, -da	fan. enthusiast
afillá, voz	husky voice
aires de Cádiz	melodies from Cádiz
alboreá°	deep song
alegría°	flamenco dance and song
Almohads	fanatic muslim sect from northern Africa
ambiente	atmosphere
andalú	andalusian dialekt for an andalusian
Andalucia la baja	lower Andalusia
autodafé	auto-da-fe
azulejo	tile

B

bailaor, bailaora	flamenco dancer, male/female
bailarín, bailarina	folk-dancer, male/female
baile por bulerías°	buleria dance
baile	dance
bandolás°	Song from Màlaga
barrio gitano	gypsy ghetto
bata de cola	flamenco dancing dress with train
bruja	wich
bulería°	fast, rhythmic flamenco dance and song

C

cabales°	deep songs
café cantante	song café
calé	gipsy in gipsy language
Calles de Cádiz, Las	the streets of Cádiz
campanilleros°	Andalusian folk dances and songs, flamenco influenced
caña°	deep song and dance
candil	oil lamp
cantante	opera singer, male/female
cantaor para baile	singer for dance
cantaor gitano	gypsy singer
cantaor, cantaora	flamenco singer
cante flamenco andaluz	flamenco song sung by a non-gypsy (payo)
cante flamenco	flamenco song
cante flamenco gitano	flamenco song sung by a gypsy (calé)
cante y baile jondo	deep, serious songs and dances coming from the depth of the heart
cante	song
cantes festeros°	festival songs
cantor, cantora	singer, not opera singer, male/female
capilla	chapel
carcelera	song from the prison
cartagenera°	deep song
caseta	small house, hut
castellanos nuevos	people from New Castil
chants	jewish songs
chorizo	strongly spiced sausage
comida	lunch
conde	count
cuadro	group

D

danzarín, danzarina	classical dancer, male/female
debla°	deep song
duende	deeply felt trance-like emotion
duque	duke

E

egipcianos	Egyptians, here denomination for gypsies
escenas andaluzas	Andalusian tales
escuela bolera	classic style Spanish dance

F

falsetas	short melodies (on guitar) as filler
fanfarrón	braggart
faraón, faraóna	in this connection expression for greatness, litt. Pharaoh, King
farruca°	flamenco influenced dance from Galicia
farruco	cocky
feria	fair

festival de flamenco	flamenco festival, usually with song, dance and guitar playing competitions
flamenco puro	genuine, pure flamenco
flamenco, flamencos	gypsy, gypsies
flamenco, un	Fleming, from Flanders
flamencologist	flamencologist, flamenco researcher

G

gaditanian	from Cádiz
garrotín°	flamenco influenced dance from Galicia
gazpacho	cold vegetable soup, typical for Andalusia
germanos	Teutons
gitano, gitana	gypsy, male/female
gitano-andaluz	gypsy-Andalusian
granadinas°	flamenco songs
grupa, a la	on the horses' loins
guajiras°	flamenco influenced songs and dances from Cuba
guitarra	guitar
guitarra latina	latin type guitar
guitarra morisca	Moorish type guitar
guitarrero	guitar builder

H

hermandad	brotherhood
hondo	deep, deeply felt
huevos a la flamenca	fried egg with strongly spiced sausage and some vegetables

I

ir con tiento	move slowly

J

jaberas°	flamenco influenced songs and dances from Cuba
jalear	stimulate, encourage
jaleo	shouts of appreciation and admiration
jamón jabugo	lightly smoked and saltet ham
jondo	deep, deeply felt
juerga	lively fiest, drinking party

L

laúd	lute
Levante	southeasterly Spain
liviana°	deep song
loco	crazy
lunar	birthmark

M

malagueña°	flamenco song and dance from Málaga
marianas°	flamenco influenced songs and dances from Andalusia
martinete°	song from the forge
media granadina°	flamenco song
melisma	tone gliding
mezquita	mosque
minera°	song from the mine
mirabrás°	flamenco song and dance
morería	moorish quarter
moriscos	Christian Moors
moros	muslims from north Africa
muleta	the red cloth of a bull-fighter

N

so seas fanfarrón	don't brag
no te pongas farruco	don't be cocky

O

opera flamenca	performance with song dance and guitar, in a bull-fighting ring

P

palmas	hand clapping
palmas y tambor	hand clapping and drum
palo seco, a	literally: to a dry stick, meaning rhythmic thumps with a stick
paseo	promenade, walk; also opening ceremony at a bullfight
payo	non-gypsy in gypsy language
petenera°	deep song and dance
picador de toros	the horseman in a bullfight who pierces his lance into the bull
pie	foot
piropo	spontaneous compliment
pitos	snapping of the fingers
plaza de toros	bullfighting arena
polo°	deep song and dance
pretencioso	pretencious
primera figura	solo artist
primitiva etapa	years 1800–1860
puente	bridge
Puertos, Los	the ports, the sea ports around Cádiz
puro	pure, authentic, genuine

R

rasgueo, rasgueado	scratching; plucking the strings of the guitar with four or five fingers consecutively
reconquista, la	the reconquest

Reyes Católicos, Los	the Catholic Royal Couple, Ferdinand and Isabel
romera°	flamenco song and dance

S

saeta°	liturgical toná
sahones	leather protection for the legs of a horseman
sefarad	Spanish jew/jewess
sefaradím	Sephardim, jews in Spain and Portugal
sefardí, sefardita	Sephardi, Spanish and Portuguese jew/jewess
seguidilla°	folk dance, couple dance, from La Mancha
Semana Santa, La	The Holy Week. Easter week
serrana°	deep song
sevillanas°	Andalusian Folk dances and songs, flamenco influenced
Siguiriya gitana°	gypsy seguiriya
siguiriya°	a toná, both song and dance
simpecado	without guilt, guiltless, just
soledad	loneliness
soníos negros	black tones (Andalusian dialect)

T

tablao	stage, podium (lit.: board)
tablao flamenco	night club, flamenco show
tangos°	flamenco songs and dances
tanguillo°	flamenco song and dance
tapa, tapas	snack, snacks
tarantas, taranto°	deep songs and dances from the Levant
taverna	inn, tavern
tiento°	deep song and dance
tío flamenco	generous person
tío, tía	uncle, aunt (within the family)
tocaor, tocaora	guitar player, male/female
toná°	first independent form of gypsy-Andalusian song
toque, el	guitar playing
torre	tower
traje campero	Andalusian riding dress
traje corto	flamenco suit for men
traje gitana	gypsy dress for women
Triana	district of Seville
trillera°	harvest song. Andalusian folk-song, flamenco influenced

V

venta	inn
verdiales°	flamenco songs and dances from Málaga
vihuela	early type of guitar
vino fino	light, dry white wine, light Sherry
volar	fly
voz afillá	husky voice

Z

Zambra	gypsy fiest, also name of "tablao" in Madrid
zambra granadina	form of gypsy dance used in the Sacromonte caves in Granada
zapateado	footwork, footwork dance
zapato	shoe

° See pages 72–78!

INDEX OF NAMES

155

Sources of illustrations
Numbers refer to pages

DRAWINGS:

Alcalá, Miguel. With kind permission of the artist himself and of Editions Filipacchi, Paris, for drawings from LE FLAMENCO ET LES GITANES, © 1987 — Front cover and pages 18, 27, 38, 57, 62.

Brazda, Jan, Stockholm — 72

Clará, José — 95

Doré, Gustave, (1833–1883). By permission of Fundación Andaluza de Flamenco, Jerez — © 1988 — Drawing by Gustave Doré, hand coloured about 1880, possibly by the artist himself — 33.

PHOTOS AND OTHER ILLUSTRATIONS:

Arenas, Luis, Seville — 123, 125, 127, 132/133, 135, 136.

Cinterco, Madrid — 37, 40, 45, 50, 54r, 81, 82, 83, 86, 111, 119.

Cramér, Casten, Lidingö — Cover back.

Guillen, Studio, Mairena del Alcor (Seville) — 54l, 70, 88, 92.

León, Mercedes, Madrid — 96, 101, 102, 108.

Lido, Paris — 110.

Mario, Foto, Lebrija (Seville) — 56l, 56r, 61, 103, 104.

Puig, Alfons, Llegat de Dansa, Barcelona — 97.

Remark, Lidingö — 12/13, 14, 21.

Robert, Marie-Noëlle, Paris — 3, 91.

Sanchez, Enrique, Alcalá de Guadaira (Seville) — 63, 64.

Stewart Gardner Museum, Isabella/Art Resource, New York — inside of cover.

Stolzenberg, Elke, Madrid — 52, 60, 140, back of jacket.

Udaeta, José de, Barcelona — 106u, 106l, 109, 114.

Acknowledgements

For all support and assistance I have been given to make it possible for me to accomplish my work with this book I am especially indebted to

D. José Manuel Allendesalazar, former Spanish Ambassador to Sweden and Mrs. Ursula Allendesalazar

Pedro Calvo-Sotelo, former Culture Counsellor at the Spanish Embassy in Stockholm

Francisco Vallecillo, Culture Counsellor, Junta de Andalucia, Seville

Antonio Zoido, Counsellor, Fundación Machado, Seville

José Joaquín Carrera Moreno, Director of Fundación Andaluza de Flamenco, Jerez

Fundación Margit y Folke Pehrzon, Madrid

The Carina Ari Memorial Foundation, Stockholm

The Rolf de Maré Memorial Foundation, Stockholm.

Barbara Thiel-Cramér

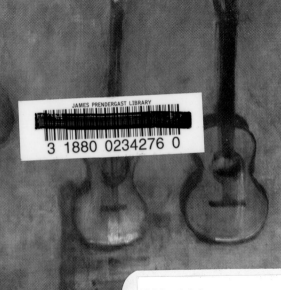

DATE DUE			

8/92